Savory Quick Breads & Muffins

Muffins, Quick Breads, Biscuits & Cornbread!

S. L. Watson

DEDICATION

To everyone who loves homemade bread but has no time to make it!

CONTENTS

INTRODUCTION

Everyone loves homemade muffins and breads. Quick breads are the easiest to make and pair well with most any meal. You do not have to be an experienced cook to make beautiful muffins, quick breads, biscuits or cornbread.

Why bother paying high prices at the store for those fancy breads? You can whip quick breads up at home and serve your family in no time. While dinner is baking, whip up a batch of biscuits or savory muffins to serve with dinner.

Who does not love biscuits? Try these savory biscuits instead of rolls at dinner time. Biscuits are not just for breakfast. Try them anytime of the day with soups, stews or salads. Nothing says lovin' like a fresh hot biscuit.

Every southerner loves cornbread and hush puppies. Try all the flavor combinations and serve them with beans, greens and a main dish for rib sticking food the whole family will enjoy!

Quick Bread Tips

Never pour cornbread batter into a cold pan. For the crispiest crust, always heat the skillet and the oil before adding the batter. When the pan is properly heated, the batter should sizzle when it hits the pan.

Every cornmeal absorbs liquids differently. For excellent cornbread, you need a pourable batter. Add additional milk if needed to make the batter the proper consistency.

Let your cornbread batter rest for 2-3 minutes before baking. The resting allows the cornbread to rise and the cornmeal to meld into the other ingredients.

Only mix a quick bread or muffin batter until the dough is moistened.. You will not have a smooth batter for most muffins and quick breads.

Do not handle biscuit dough anymore than necessary. Over working or handling the dough will make for tough biscuits.

Place biscuits with the sides touching to make the biscuits rise higher.

When cutting biscuits, do not twist the biscuit cutter. Push the cutter straight down. This will prevent the outside of your biscuits from being tough and uneven.

1 MUFFINS

Southern Cornmeal Muffins

Makes 12 muffins

1 cup all purpose flour
1 tbs. baking powder
1/8 tsp. salt
1/8 tsp. black pepper
1 cup yellow or white plain cornmeal
2 eggs
1 cup whole milk
9 tbs. vegetable oil or bacon drippings
1 cup whole kernel corn, cooked

Do not use muffin liners for this recipe. Grease your muffin cups with 3 tablespoons vegetable oil or bacon drippings. Place about 1 teaspoon of oil in each muffin cup.

Preheat the oven to 400°. For crispy muffins, the muffin tin needs to be hot before you place the batter in the muffin tin. Once the muffin tin is greased, place the muffin tin in the oven for 2-3 minutes. You will know the muffin tin is ready when the batter hits the oil and it sizzles.

In a mixing bowl, add the all purpose flour, baking powder, salt, black pepper, cornmeal and whole kernel corn. Stir until well mixed. Add the eggs, 6 tablespoons vegetable oil or bacon drippings and the milk. Mix only until well combined. Spoon the batter into the prepared muffin tin filling the muffin cups about 2/3 full.

Bake for 15-20 minutes or until the center of the muffin is firm and the muffin is golden brown. Remove the muffins from the pan and serve hot with butter or sorghum.

Serving Suggestion: The muffins are great with soups, stews, chili or beans. Use them for breakfast served with bacon or sausage and fresh fruit.

Ham & Cheese Muffins

Makes 12 muffins

2 cups all purpose flour
1 tbs. baking powder
1/8 tsp. salt
1/8 tsp. black pepper
1 cup finely chopped cooked ham
1 1/2 cups shredded sharp cheddar cheese
2 eggs
1 cup whole milk
6 tbs. melted unsalted butter or vegetable oil

Preheat the oven to 400°. Spray a 12 cup muffin tin with non stick cooking spray. In a mixing bowl, add the all purpose flour, baking powder, salt and black pepper. Stir until well combined.

Add the eggs, melted butter and whole milk. Mix only until combined. Gently fold in the ham and 1 cup shredded cheese. Spoon the batter into the prepared muffin tin filling the muffin cups about 2/3 full. Bake for 15-18 minutes or until the center of the muffins are done and the tops lightly browned. Remove the muffins from the oven. Sprinkle the remaining 1/2 cup sharp cheddar cheese over the top of the muffins.

Let the muffins rest in the pan for 5 minutes to melt the cheese on top. Serve the muffins warm.

Serving Suggestion: These muffins are delicious for breakfast with fried eggs. I like to serve them as sandwiches. Split the muffins in half. Place a piece of cooked ham and a slice of tomato and green bell pepper on the bottom half of the muffin. Place the top of the muffin over the filling and serve. You can replace the ham with cooked bacon or sausage if desired. Excellent with a hearty garden salad for lunch or dinner. Serve with a light soup for a wonderful lunch.

Bacon & Egg Breakfast Muffins

Makes 12 muffins

2 cups self rising flour
2 tsp. granulated sugar
1 tsp. dry mustard
3/4 cup shredded cheddar cheese
1 egg
3/4 cup whole milk
1/4 cup vegetable oil
2 hard boiled eggs, diced
4 slices bacon, cooked and crumbled

Preheat the oven to 400°. Spray a 12 cup muffin tin with non stick cooking spray. In a mixing bowl, add the self rising flour, granulated sugar, dry mustard and cheddar cheese. Stir until well blended.

In a separate bowl, add the egg, milk and vegetable oil. Whisk until well blended. Add the egg and milk mixture to the dry ingredients. Stir only until the batter is moistened and combined.

Spoon the batter into the prepared muffin cups filling the cups only 1/3 full. Sprinkle the hard boiled eggs and bacon over the batter. Spoon the remaining batter over the bacon and eggs. Fill the muffin cups about 2/3 full. Bake for 18-25 minutes or until the muffins are firm and golden brown. Remove the muffins from the oven and cool the muffins for 5 minutes in the pan. Remove the muffins from the pan and serve hot.

Serving suggestion: They are delicious by themselves but extra good with butter, jam or syrup. Serve them with a fresh fruit platter, ham slices and yogurt for a delightful brunch.

Onion Muffins

Makes 12 muffins

1 egg, beaten
1/3 cup vegetable oil
3/4 cup milk
1 cup self rising flour
1 cup old fashioned rolled oats
1/4 cup granulated sugar
1/2 cup chopped onion
3/4 cup shredded sharp cheddar cheese
1/4 cup chopped pecans

Preheat the oven to 400°. Spray a muffin tin with non stick cooking spray. In a mixing bowl, add the milk and oats. Let the oats sit in the milk for 5 minutes. Add the egg, vegetable oil and onion. Whisk until well combined.

Stir in the self rising flour, granulated sugar, cheddar cheese and the pecans. Mix only until blended. Spoon the batter into the prepared muffin tin filling the muffin cups about 2/3 full. Bake for 15-18 minutes or until the muffins are golden brown. Let the muffins rest in the pan for 5 minutes before serving.

Serving suggestion: Serve with eggs and bacon, sausage or ham for breakfast. The muffins go well with most any meat or casserole dish for supper. They are excellent with soups and stews.

Savory Crab Muffins

Makes 8 -10 muffins

1 lb. cooked crab meat, chopped
10 slices toasted bread, crumbled
1/2 cup onion, finely chopped
1/2 cup celery, finely chopped
2 eggs
1 tsp. yellow prepared mustard
1 tsp. Worcestershire sauce
1 tbs. unsalted butter, melted
1/4 to 1/2 cup whole milk

Preheat the oven to 350°. Spray your muffin tin with non stick cooking spray. In a skillet over medium low heat, add the butter, onion and celery. Saute the onion and celery until they are softened or about 4 minutes. Remove the pan from the heat.

In a mixing bowl, add the crab meat, eggs, mustard, Worcestershire sauce and crumbled bread. Add the butter, onion and celery. Stir until well combined. If the stuffing is dry, add 1/4 cup milk. Only add enough milk to make a moist stuffing. You do not want the stuffing to be soupy.

Spoon the mixture into the prepared muffin cups. Fill the muffin cups to the top. Bake for 30-45 minutes or until a toothpick inserted in the center of the muffins comes out clean. Remove the muffins from the oven and let them rest in the muffin pan for 5 minutes before removing them from the pan. Serve warm.

Serving suggestion: Serve with remoulade sauce or use a mini muffin tin and serve the muffins as appetizers. The muffins are great with a seafood chowder.

Turkey Dressing Muffins

These muffins do not use turkey but taste like southern dressing. They are delicious with turkey.

Makes 12-14 muffins

2 cups self rising white cornmeal
3/4 cup finely chopped onion
3/4 cup finely chopped celery
1 tbs. granulated sugar
1 tsp. poultry seasoning
1/4 tsp. rubbed sage
2 eggs
1 cup whole milk
1/4 cup vegetable oil

If you do not have poultry seasoning on hand, substitute 1/2 teaspoon rubbed sage, 1/4 teaspoon black pepper, 1/8 teaspoon thyme and 1/8 teaspoon salt for the poultry seasoning.

Preheat the oven to 425°. Spray a 12 cup muffin tin with non stick cooking spray. In a mixing bowl, add the cornmeal, onion, celery, granulated sugar, poultry seasoning and sage. Stir until well combined.

In a separate bowl, add the eggs, milk and vegetable oil. Whisk until well combined. Pour the egg and milk mixture into the dry ingredients. Mix only until the batter is moistened and combined. Spoon the batter into the prepared muffin tin filling the muffin cups a little more than 2/3 full. Bake for 16-20 minutes or until the muffins are firm and golden brown.

Remove the muffins from the oven and let the muffins cool for 5 minutes before removing them from the pan.

Serving suggestion: Serve with turkey and cranberry sauce for a quick dinner. The muffins go well with chicken or most any fowl. Leftover muffins make excellent stuffing.

Cranberry & Brie Muffins

Makes 12 muffins

2 cups all purpose flour
1 tbs. baking powder
1/2 tsp. baking soda
1/8 tsp. salt
3/4 cup chilled Brie, finely diced
2 eggs
1 cup sour cream
6 tbs. vegetable oil
4 tbs. cranberry jelly

Preheat the oven to 400°. Spray a 12 cup muffin tin with non stick cooking spray. Spray the muffin tin well or these muffins will stick. Do not use muffin liners for this recipe.

In a mixing bowl, add the all purpose flour, baking powder, baking soda and salt. Stir until well blended. In a separate mixing bowl, add the eggs, sour cream and vegetable oil. Whisk until well blended. Add the mixture to the dry ingredients. Mix only until combined. Gently fold in the chilled Brie cheese.

Fill the muffin cups about 1/3 full with half of the batter. Drop about a teaspoon of the jelly in the center of each muffin. Spoon the remaining batter over the jelly filling the muffin cups about 2/3 full. Bake for 15-18 minutes or until the center of the muffins are firm and the muffins are golden brown. Remove the muffins from the oven and let the muffins rest in the pan for 5 minutes before removing them from the pan.

Serving suggestion: Serve with fresh fruit and oatmeal for a hearty breakfast. The muffins are great with any salad or soup for lunch. Split the muffins open and serve with a scoop of vanilla ice cream on the bottom half of the muffin. Place the top half of the muffin over the ice cream. Drizzle with warm cranberry jelly for a delicious dessert.

Garlic & Cream Cheese Muffins

Makes 12 muffins

2 cups all purpose flour
1 tbs. baking powder
1/2 tsp. baking soda
1/8 tsp. salt
1/8 tsp. black pepper
2 eggs
2/3 cup sour cream
6 tbs. vegetable oil
3/4 cup cream cheese with garlic, softened

Spray a 12 cup muffin tin with non stick cooking spray. Preheat the oven to 400°. In a mixing bowl, add the all purpose flour, baking powder, baking soda, salt and black pepper. Stir until well combined.

In a separate bowl, add the eggs, sour cream, vegetable oil and cream cheese. Stir until well combined. Spoon the mixture into the dry ingredients. Mix only until combined and the batter is moistened.

Spoon the batter into the prepared muffin tin filling the muffin cups about 2/3 full. Bake for 15-18 minutes or until the muffins are firm to the touch and lightly browned. Remove the muffins from the oven and let the muffins rest in the pan for 5 minutes before removing them from the pan.

Serving suggestion: Serve with spaghetti, lasagna, soups or salads. Make a sandwich with the split muffins using your favorite deli meats.

Smoked Salmon Muffins

Makes 12 muffins

2 cups all purpose flour
1 tbs. baking powder
1/8 tsp. salt
2 eggs
1 cup whole milk
6 tbs. vegetable oil
3/4 cup smoked salmon, finely chopped
2 tbs. fresh dill, minced

Spray a 12 cup muffin tin with non stick cooking spray. Preheat the oven to 400°. In a mixing bowl, add the all purpose flour, baking powder and salt. Whisk until well combined. Add the eggs, milk, vegetable oil and dill. Mix only until combined. Gently fold in the salmon. Spoon the batter into the prepared muffin tin filling the muffin cups about 2/3 full.

Bake for 15-18 minutes or until the muffins are firm to the touch and golden brown. Let the muffins cool for 5 minutes before removing them from the muffin tin.

Serving suggestion: Serve warm with dill cream cheese and additional slices of smoked salmon for a light lunch, breakfast or snack.

Cheddar & Chive Muffins

Makes 12 muffins

2 1/2 cups all purpose flour
1 tbs. baking powder
1/4 tsp. salt
1/4 tsp. black pepper
1 1/2 cups sharp cheddar cheese, shredded
4 tbs. fresh chives, minced
2 eggs
1 cup whole milk
6 tbs. melted unsalted butter or vegetable oil
3 tbs. unsalted butter, cut into small pieces

Preheat the oven to 400°. Spray a 12 cup muffin tin with non stick cooking spray. Do not use muffin liners for this recipe. In a mixing bowl, add 2 cups all purpose flour, baking powder, 1/8 teaspoon salt, 1/8 teaspoon black pepper, 1 1/4 cups cheddar cheese and the chives. Whisk until well combined.

Add the eggs, whole milk and 6 tablespoons melted butter. Mix only until combined. Spoon the batter into the prepared muffin tin filling the muffin cups about 2/3 full.

In a small bowl, add 1/2 cup all purpose flour. 1/8 teaspoon salt, 1/8 teaspoon black pepper and 3 tablespoons butter. Use your fingers and work the butter into the all purpose flour. Add the remaining 1/4 cup cheddar cheese and mix only until combined. Sprinkle this mixture over the top of each muffin. Bake for 15-18 minutes or until the muffins are done in the center and golden brown.

Remove the muffins from the oven and let them cool in the pan for 5 minutes before removing the muffins from the pan.

Serving suggestion: These muffins are an excellent base for taco meat. Spoon the taco meat over split muffins and top each muffin with sour cream, fresh diced tomatoes, green onions and sour cream. Serve with a deli platter of meats and cheeses along with fresh fruit for a refreshing lunch or dinner.

Parmesan Pecan Muffins

Makes 12 muffins

2 cups all purpose flour
1 tbs. baking powder
1/8 tsp. salt
1/8 tsp. black pepper
1 cup freshly grated Parmesan cheese
3/4 cup finely chopped pecans
2 eggs
1 cup whole milk
6 tbs. vegetable oil

Spray a 12 cup muffin tin with non stick cooking spray. Preheat the oven to 400°. In a mixing bowl, add the all purpose flour, baking powder, salt, black pepper, 3/4 cup Parmesan cheese and 1/2 cup pecans. Whisk until well blended.

Add the eggs, whole milk and vegetable oil. Mix only until the batter is combined and moistened. Spoon the batter into the prepared muffin tin filling the muffin cups about 2/3 full. Sprinkle the remaining 1/4 cup Parmesan cheese and 1/4 cup pecans over the top of the muffins.

Bake for 16-20 minutes or until the top of the muffins are firm to the touch and golden brown. Remove the muffins from the oven and cool the muffins for 5 minutes before removing them from the pan.

Serving suggestion: These muffins are great with any meal. We like them with Italian dishes instead of garlic bread. Serve the muffins for breakfast with bacon and eggs. Extremely tasty for lunch with soup and salad.

Gourmet Zucchini Muffins

Makes 12 muffins

1 1/2 cups raw zucchini, finely diced
2 cups all purpose flour
1 tbs. baking powder
1/8 tsp. salt
2 tbs. sesame seeds, optional
1/2 tsp. dried Italian seasonings
2 eggs
1 cup plain yogurt
6 tbs. vegetable oil
1/2 cup freshly grated Parmesan cheese

Preheat the oven to 350°. Spray a 12 cup muffin tin with non stick cooking spray. In a mixing bowl, add the all purpose flour, zucchini, baking powder, salt and Italian seasoning. Whisk until well blended.

Add the eggs, yogurt and vegetable oil. Whisk only until the batter is combined and moistened. Spoon the batter into the prepared muffin tin filling the muffin cups about 2/3 full. Sprinkle the Parmesan cheese and sesame seeds across the muffins. Bake for 18-20 minutes or until the muffins are firm to the touch and golden brown.

Remove the muffins from the oven and let the muffins cool for 5 minutes before removing them from the pan.

Serving suggestion: Serve with ham, pork chops or spaghetti. Split the muffins in half and use the muffins as "slider buns" for hamburgers. Serve with eggs and sausage for breakfast. Wonderful with a soup or salad for a light lunch or dinner.

Goat Cheese Muffins

Makes 12 muffins

2 cups all purpose flour
1 tbs. baking powder
1/8 tsp. salt
1 cup green onions, finely chopped
2 eggs
3/4 cup goat cheese, finely chopped
1 cup whole milk
6 tbs. unsalted melted butter

Spray a 12 cup muffin tin with non stick cooking spray. Preheat the oven to 400°. In a mixing bowl, add the all purpose flour, baking powder, salt, green onions and goat cheese. Stir until combined.

Add the eggs, milk and melted butter. Mix only until the muffins are combined and moistened. Spoon the batter into the prepared muffin tin filling the muffin cups about 2/3 full. Bake for 15-18 minutes or until the muffins are firm to the touch and golden brown. Remove the muffins from the oven and let the muffins cool for 5 minutes before removing them from the pan.

Serving suggestion: Serve with pork, chicken or beef for lunch or dinner. Perfect accompaniment to a hearty soup.

Spinach Muffins

Makes 12 muffins

10 oz. pkg. frozen spinach, thawed and all moisture removed
6 tbs. vegetable oil
1 onion, finely chopped
2 cups all purpose flour
1 tbs. baking powder
1/8 tsp. salt
1/8 tsp. black pepper
1/4 tsp. ground nutmeg
2 eggs
1 cup whole milk
1/2 cup freshly grated Parmesan cheese

Preheat the oven to 350°. Spray a 12 cup muffin tin with non stick cooking spray. In a mixing bowl, add the all purpose flour, baking powder, nutmeg, salt and black pepper. Whisk until well blended.

In a separate bowl, add the spinach, eggs, onion, vegetable oil and milk. Mix until well combined. Spoon this mixture into the dry ingredients. Mix only until the batter is combined and moistened.

Spoon the batter into the prepared muffin tin filling the muffin cups about 2/3 full. Sprinkle the Parmesan cheese across the top of the muffins. Bake for 18-20 minutes or until the muffins are firm to the touch and golden brown. Remove the muffins from the oven and let the muffins cool for 5 minutes before removing them from the pan.

Serving suggestion: Serve with marinated artichokes and black olives. Great with soup and a salad. Delicious with most meats and casseroles.

Parsley Shrimp Muffins

Makes 12 muffins

2 cups all purpose flour
1 tbs. baking powder
1/8 tsp. salt
1/8 tsp. black pepper
2 eggs
1 cup whole milk
6 tbs. unsalted butter, melted
3 tbs. fresh parsley, chopped
1 cup cooked shrimp, finely chopped

Preheat the oven to 400°. Spray a 12 cup muffin tin with non stick cooking spray. In a mixing bowl, add the all purpose flour, baking powder, parsley, salt and black pepper. Whisk until well combined.

Add the eggs, milk and melted butter. Mix only until combined and the batter is moistened. Gently fold in the shrimp. Spoon the batter into the prepared muffin tin filling the muffin cups about 2/3 full. Bake for 15-18 minutes or until the muffins are firm to the touch and golden brown. Remove the muffins from the oven and let the muffins cool for 5 minutes before removing them from the pan.

Serving suggestion: Serve with cream cheese, spread with garlic butter or make into mini muffins and serve as an appetizer. The muffins pair well with most any seafood or chowder. Serve with a salad for a light meal.

Chorizo Muffins

Makes 12 muffins

2 cups all purpose flour
1 tbs. baking powder
1/8 tsp. salt
1 tsp. paprika
1 cup green bell pepper, finely chopped
2 eggs
1 cup whole milk
6 tbs. vegetable oil
1 garlic clove, minced
3/4 cup chorizo sausage, cooked and finely chopped

Preheat the oven to 350°. Spray a 12 cup muffin tin with non stick cooking spray. In a mixing bowl, add the all purpose flour, baking powder, salt and paprika. Whisk until well combined.

In a separate bowl, add the green bell pepper, eggs, milk, vegetable oil, garlic and chorizo sausage. Stir until well blended. Pour the mixture into the dry ingredients. Mix only until the batter is combined and moistened.

Spoon the batter into the prepared muffin tin filling the muffin cups about 2/3 full. Bake for 18-22 minutes or until the muffins are firm to the touch and golden brown. Remove the muffins from the oven and let the muffins cool for 5 minutes before removing them from the pan.

Serving suggestion: Spread cream cheese across split muffins. Serve with a spicy chili or soup. Excellent with red beans and rice.

Tuna & Black Olive Muffins

Makes 12 muffins

2 cups all purpose flour
1 tbs. baking powder
1/8 tsp. salt
1/8 tsp. black pepper
1/2 cup black olives, diced
2 eggs
1 cup whole milk
6 tbs. vegetable oil
1 3/4 cups canned tuna, drained

Preheat the oven to 400°. Spray a 12 cup muffin tin with non stick cooking spray. In a mixing bowl, add the all purpose flour, baking powder, salt and black pepper. Whisk until well combined.

Add the eggs, whole milk and vegetable oil. Mix only until combined and the batter is moistened. Gently fold in the black olives and tuna. Spoon the batter into the prepared muffin tin filling the muffin cups about 2/3 full. Bake for 15-18 minutes or until the muffins are firm to the touch and golden brown. Remove the muffins from the oven and let the muffins cool for 5 minutes before removing them from the pan.

Serving suggestion: Spread the muffins with cream cheese and serve with a bowl of tomato soup for lunch. The muffins are very good served with a hearty salad or pasta salad for lunch or dinner.

Zesty Chicken & Corn Muffins

Makes 12 muffins

6 tbs. vegetable oil
1 onion, finely chopped
3/4 cup cooked chicken, finely chopped
2 cups all purpose flour
1 tbs. baking powder
1/8 tsp. salt
1/4 tsp. cayenne pepper
2 eggs
1 cup whole milk
1/2 cup whole kernel corn, cooked
1/8 tsp. paprika

Preheat the oven to 400°. Spray a 12 cup muffin tin with non stick cooking spray. Do not use muffin liners for this recipe.

In a mixing bowl, add the all purpose flour, baking powder, salt, cayenne pepper and paprika. Whisk until well combined.

In a separate bowl, add the vegetable oil, eggs, milk, chicken, onion and corn. Stir until well blended. Add the mixture to the dry ingredients. Mix only until the batter is combined and moistened.

Spoon the batter into the prepared muffin tin filling the muffin cups about 2/3 full. Bake for 15-18 minutes or until the muffins are firm to the touch and golden brown. Remove the muffins from the oven and let the muffins cool for 5 minutes before removing them from the pan.

Serving suggestion: Serve with fried chicken and coleslaw. Wonderful with chicken noodle soup or a salad.

Bacon Onion Muffins

Makes 12 muffins

1 1/4 cups cooked & crumbled bacon
6 tbs. vegetable oil
1 onion, finely chopped
2 cups all purpose flour
1 tbs. baking powder
1/8 tsp. salt
2 eggs
1 cup whole milk

Preheat the oven to 350°. Spray a 12 cup muffin tin with non stick cooking spray. In a mixing bowl, add the all purpose flour, baking powder and salt. Whisk until well combined.

Add the eggs, onion, vegetable oil, bacon and milk. Mix only until the batter is combined and moistened. Spoon the batter into the prepared muffin tin filling the muffin cups about 2/3 full. Bake for 18-22 minutes or until the muffins are firm to the touch and golden brown. Remove the muffins from the oven and let the muffins cool for 5 minutes before removing them from the pan.

Serving suggestion: Serve with eggs and fresh fruit for breakfast. Split the muffins open and spread with mayonnaise. Place tomato and avocado slices on each half of the muffin for an open face sandwich. Serve with soup, salad or hearty vegetable platter for dinner.

Caramelized Onion Muffins

Makes 12 muffins

6 tbs. vegetable oil
3 onions, finely chopped
1 tbs. red wine vinegar
2 tsp. granulated sugar
2 cups all purpose flour
1 tbs. baking powder
1/8 tsp. salt
1/8 tsp. black pepper
2 eggs
1 cup whole milk

In a skillet over medium low heat, add 3 tablespoons vegetable oil. Add the onions and saute the onions for 7-8 minutes. The onions should be golden brown when ready. Add the red wine vinegar and granulated sugar. Stir until combined. Cook for 2 minutes.

Preheat the oven to 350°. Spray a 12 cup muffin tin with non stick cooking spray. In a mixing bowl, add the all purpose flour, baking powder, salt and black pepper. Whisk until combined.

In a separate bowl, add the onions and any remaining oil from the skillet, 3 tablespoons vegetable oil, eggs and milk. Whisk until well combined. Pour this mixture into the dry ingredients. Mix only until the batter is moistened and combined.

Spoon the batter into the prepared muffin tin filling the muffin cups about 2/3 full. Bake for 15-18 minutes or until the muffins are firm to the touch and golden brown. Remove the muffins from the oven and let the muffins cool for 5 minutes before removing them from the pan.

Serving suggestion: Serve with crispy bacon and eggs for breakfast. Split the muffins and use as bread for mini sandwiches. The muffins go well with most meats and casseroles.

Asparagus Sour Cream Muffins

Makes 12 muffins

6 tbs. vegetable oil
8 oz. fresh asparagus, roasted and diced
2 cups all purpose flour
1 tbs. baking powder
1/8 tsp. salt
1/8 tsp. black pepper
2 eggs
1 cup sour cream
1/3 cup shredded cheddar cheese
1/4 cup grated Parmesan cheese

Preheat the oven to 350°. Spray a 12 cup muffin tin with non stick cooking spray. In a mixing bowl, add the all purpose flour, baking powder, salt and black pepper.

In a separate bowl, add the asparagus, eggs, sour cream, vegetable oil and cheddar cheese. Mix together until well combined. Pour the mixture into the dry ingredients. Mix only until the batter is moistened and combined.

Spoon the batter into the prepared muffin tin filling the muffin cups about 2/3 full. Sprinkle the Parmesan cheese across the top of the muffins. Bake for 18-20 minutes or until the muffins are firm to the touch and golden brown. Remove the muffins from the oven and let the muffins cool for 5 minutes before removing them from the pan.

Serving suggestion: Serve with ham slices and a cheese sauce to spread across the muffins. The muffins are great with soup and salad. Serve with Canadian bacon and fried eggs for breakfast.

Pepperoni & Tomato Muffins

Makes 12 muffins

2 cups all purpose flour
1 tbs. baking powder
1/8 tsp. salt
1/8 tsp. black pepper
1 tsp. dried oregano
1/2 cup sun dried tomatoes, finely chopped
6 tbs. vegetable oil
1 garlic clove, minced
1/2 cup pepperoni, finely chopped
1 cup whole milk
2 eggs
1/2 cup freshly grated Parmesan cheese

If using sun dried tomatoes that are not packed in oil, you will need to rehydrate the tomatoes. Place 1/2 cup sun dried tomatoes in a mixing bowl. Pour 2 cups boiling water over the tomatoes. Let the tomatoes soak for 1 hour. Use as directed in the recipe.

Preheat the oven to 350°. Spray a 12 cup muffin tin with non stick cooking spray. In a mixing bowl, add the all purpose flour, baking powder, salt, black pepper, oregano and dried tomatoes. Whisk until blended.

In a separate bowl, add the eggs, garlic, pepperoni, milk and vegetable oil. Whisk until well blended. Spoon the mixture into the dry ingredients. Mix only until the batter is blended and moistened.

Spoon the batter into the prepared muffin tin filling the muffin cups about 2/3 full. Sprinkle the Parmesan cheese across the tops of the muffins. Bake for 18-20 minutes or until the muffins are firm to the touch and golden brown. Remove the muffins from the oven and let the muffins cool for 5 minutes before removing them from the pan.

Serving suggestion: Serve with marinara sauce for dipping. Split the muffins in half and top each half with a slice of mozzarella cheese. Broil the muffins for 1 minute or until the mozzarella cheese is melted.

Tomato Basil Muffins

Makes 12 muffins

2 cups all purpose flour
1 tbs. baking powder
1/8 tsp. salt
3/4 cup sun dried tomatoes, finely chopped
6 tbs. vegetable oil
2 eggs
1 cup whole milk
4 tbs. fresh chopped basil leaves
1 garlic clove, minced
1/4 cup Parmesan cheese, grated

If using sun dried tomatoes that are not packed in oil, you will need to rehydrate the tomatoes. Place 1/2 cup sun dried tomatoes in a mixing bowl. Pour 2 cups boiling water over the tomatoes. Let the tomatoes soak for 1 hour. Use as directed in the recipe.

Preheat the oven to 350°. Spray a 12 cup muffin tin with non stick cooking spray. In a mixing bowl, add the all purpose flour, baking powder, salt, garlic, tomatoes and basil. Stir until blended.

In a separate bowl, add the eggs, vegetable oil, milk and Parmesan cheese. Whisk until combined. Pour the mixture into the dry ingredients. Mix only until the batter is moistened and combined.

Spoon the batter into the prepared muffin tin filling the muffin cups about 2/3 full. Bake for 16-20 minutes or until the muffins are firm to the touch and golden brown. Remove the muffins from the oven and let the muffins cool for 5 minutes before removing them from the pan.

Serving suggestion: Delicious with most any meat dish or casserole. Serve with soups and salads. Split the muffins in half and use as the base for pizza crust. Place pepperoni, black olives and a slice of mozzarella cheese on each muffin half. Broil for 2 minutes or until the cheese is melted and the pepperoni hot.

Pesto Muffins

Makes 12 muffins

2 cups all purpose flour
1 tbs. baking powder
1/8 tsp. salt
1/4 cup pine nuts
2 eggs
3/4 cup whole milk
6 tbs. vegetable oil
6 tbs. pesto
1/2 cup freshly grated Parmesan cheese

Preheat the oven to 350°. Spray a 12 cup muffin tin with non stick cooking spray. In a mixing bowl, add the all purpose flour, baking powder, salt and pine nuts. Stir until well blended.

In a separate bowl, add the eggs, milk, vegetable oil, pesto and 1/4 cup Parmesan cheese. Whisk until well blended. Pour the mixture into the dry ingredients. Mix only until the batter is moistened and combined.

Spoon the batter into the prepared muffin tin filling the muffin cups about 2/3 full. Sprinkle the remaining 1/4 cup Parmesan cheese across the tops of the muffins. Bake for 18-20 minutes or until the muffins are firm to the touch and golden brown. Remove the muffins from the oven and let the muffins cool for 5 minutes before removing them from the pan.

Serving suggestion: Serve with herb flavored cream cheeses, goat cheese or a slice of sharp cheddar cheese. The muffins are great with any tomato based casserole or soup.

Whole Wheat Muffins

These muffins are just too good to be left out.

Makes 12 muffins

1 cup all purpose flour
2 tsp. baking powder
1 tsp. salt
1 cup whole wheat flour
1/4 cup molasses
1 egg, beaten
1 cup whole milk
1/4 cup unsalted butter, melted

Preheat the oven to 400°. Spray a 12 cup muffin tin with non stick cooking spray. In a mixing bowl, add the all purpose flour, baking powder, salt and whole wheat flour. Stir until well combined.

In a separate bowl, add the molasses, egg, milk and butter. Stir until well combined. Pour the wet ingredients into the dry ingredients. Mix only until the batter is moistened. The batter may be lumpy.

Spoon the batter into the muffin tin filling the cups about 2/3 full. Bake for 20-25 minutes or until the muffins are springy when touched and golden brown. Remove the muffins from the pan and cool the muffins in the pan for 5 minutes before serving.

Serving suggestion: Serve with any meal instead of rolls. They are delicious served with butter or flavored butters and jams.

You can add 2 teaspoons of your favorite herbs to the batter. You can add 1 cup of any combination of meat and cheese to the muffins for heartier muffins. You may need to add a tablespoon or two additional milk if adding ingredients.

Carrot Parsley Muffins

Makes 12 muffins

2 cups all purpose flour
1 tbs. baking powder
1/8 tsp. salt
1 cup grated carrots
3 tbs. fresh minced parsley
2 eggs
1 cup whole milk
6 tbs. vegetable oil

Preheat the oven to 350°. Spray a 12 cup muffin tin with non stick cooking spray. In a mixing bowl, add the all purpose flour, baking powder, salt, carrots and parsley. Mix until well combined.

Add the eggs, milk and vegetable oil. Stir only until the batter is combined and moistened. Spoon the batter into the prepared muffin tin filling the muffin cups about 2/3 full. Bake for 16-18 minutes or until the muffins are firm to the touch and golden brown. Remove the muffins from the oven and let the muffins cool for 5 minutes before removing them from the pan.

Serving suggestion: Serve with any meat or casserole. Excellent with soups and salads. Make a great between meal snack with fresh fruit.

Cheesy Herb Muffins

Makes 12 muffins

1/4 cup minced onion
1/4 cup minced parsley
2 tsp. dill seed
1 tbs. fresh thyme, minced
2 tsp. minced garlic
2 cups all purpose flour
2 tbs. granulated sugar
2 tsp. baking powder
1 tsp. baking soda
1/4 tsp. salt
1/2 tsp. dried dill
1/8 tsp. black pepper
1/3 cup unsalted butter
1 cup cheddar cheese, diced
1/4 cup Parmesan cheese, grated
1 egg
1 cup whole milk

Preheat the oven to 400°. Spray a 12 cup muffin tin with non stick cooking spray. In a mixing bowl, add the minced onion, parsley, dill seed, thyme, garlic, all purpose flour, granulated sugar, baking powder, baking soda, salt, dill, black pepper and Parmesan cheese. Stir until well combined. Add the butter and using your fingers, work the butter into the dry ingredients. You should still see tiny pieces of the butter when done.

In a small bowl, add the egg and milk. Whisk until well combined. Add the egg and milk along with the cheddar cheese to the dry ingredients. Mix only until the batter is moistened.

Spoon the batter into the muffin tin filling the cups about 2/3 full. Bake for 12-15 minutes or until the muffins are firm to the touch and golden brown. Remove the muffins from the pan and let them rest in the pan for 5 minutes. Remove the muffins from the pan and serve warm or cold.

Serving suggestion: Serve with eggs and bacon for breakfast. Great with Italian dishes or most any casserole.

Cumin & Parmesan Muffins

Makes 12 muffins

2 1/2 cups self rising flour
1 tsp. granulated sugar
1/4 tsp. salt
1 cup freshly grated Parmesan cheese
3 1/2 tbs. unsalted butter, melted
1 1/2 cups whole milk
1 egg
2 tsp. ground cumin
1 tsp. toasted cumin seeds, optional

Preheat the oven to 375°. Spray a 12 count muffin tin with non stick cooking spray. In a mixing bowl, add the self rising flour, granulated sugar, salt, Parmesan cheese, ground cumin and cumin seeds. Stir until well blended.

Add the egg, milk and melted butter. Mix only until the batter is moistened. Spoon the batter into the prepared muffin tin filling the cups about 2/3 full. Bake for 15-20 minutes or until the center of the muffins test clean with a toothpick and are lightly browned.

Remove the muffins from the oven and cool for 5 minutes before removing the muffins from the pan.

Onion & Chive Muffins

Makes 12 muffins

1 onion, finely chopped
2 tbs. unsalted butter
1 1/2 cups all purpose flour
1 tbs. granulated sugar
1 1/2 tsp. baking powder
1/2 tsp. baking soda
1/2 tsp. salt
1 cup buttermilk
1/3 cup fresh minced chives
1/4 cup vegetable oil
1 egg

Preheat the oven to 350°. Spray a 12 cup muffin tin with non stick cooking spray. In a skillet over medium low heat, add the butter and onion. Saute the onion for 4-5 minutes or until the onion is soft and tender. Remove the skillet from the heat.

Add the buttermilk, vegetable oil and egg to the skillet. Whisk until well blended. Add the all purpose flour, granulated sugar, baking powder, baking soda , salt and chives. Mix only until the batter is moistened and combined. Spoon the batter into the prepared muffin tin filling the muffin cups about 2/3 full. Bake for 14-18 minutes or until the muffins are firm and golden brown. Remove the muffins from the pan and cool for 10 minutes.

Note: Adding 1 cup finely diced roast beef or ham is delicious in these muffins.

Serving suggestion: Serve with any meat, main dish or casserole. Delicious spread with cheese or herb flavored cream cheese.

Queso Fresco Muffins with Green Chiles

Makes 12 muffins

1/4 cup chopped onion
1/4 cup chopped green bell pepper
4 tbs. vegetable oil
2 1/2 cups all purpose flour
2 tsp. baking powder
1 tsp. salt
1 tbs. granulated sugar
4 oz. queso fresco, crumbled
1 tbs. diced red pimento
2 tbs. diced green chiles
2 eggs
1 1/2 cups whole milk
5 tbs. chopped green onion

Preheat the oven to 350°. Spray a 12 cup muffin tin with non stick cooking spray. In a skillet over medium low heat, add the onion, green bell pepper, vegetable oil and 3 tablespoons green onion. Saute the vegetables about 5 minutes or until they are tender. Remove the pan from the heat.

Add the red pimento, green chiles, eggs and whole milk to the skillet. Mix until well combined. Add the all purpose flour, baking powder, salt, sugar and queso fresco to the skillet. Mix only until the batter is moistened.

Spoon the batter into the muffin tin filling the muffin cups about 2/3 full. Sprinkle the remaining green onions over the top of the muffins. Bake for 14-18 minutes or until the muffins are firm and lightly browned. Remove the pan from the oven and cool the muffins for 10 minutes before removing them from the pan.

Serving suggestion: Serve with sausage, bacon and eggs for breakfast. Great with soups and salads. The muffins go well with most casseroles.

Sausage & Oat Muffins

Makes 12 muffins

1 1/4 cups all purpose flour
3/4 cup old fashioned oats
2 tsp. baking powder
1 tsp. baking soda
1/2 tsp. salt
1 tsp. garlic powder
1/3 cup unsalted butter, melted
2 eggs
1 cup whole milk
1 cup cooked and crumbled pork sausage
2 tsp. sharp cheddar cheese, shredded

Preheat the oven to 350°. Spray a 12 cup muffin tin with non stick cooking spray. In a mixing bowl, add the all purpose flour, oats, baking powder, baking soda, salt and garlic powder. Stir until well blended.

In a separate bowl, add the butter, eggs, milk and sausage. Stir until well combined. Add the wet ingredients to the flour mixture. Stir only until moistened. Spoon the batter into the prepared muffin cups filling the muffin cups about 2/3 full. Sprinkle the cheddar cheese across the top of each muffin. Bake for 15-18 minutes or until the muffins are firm and lightly browned. Remove the muffins from the oven and cool the muffins for 10 minutes before removing them from the pan. Serve warm

Serving suggestion: Serve with any soup or stew, meat or casserole.

Blue Cornmeal Muffins with Green Chiles

Makes 12 muffins

1 cup plain blue cornmeal
1 cup all purpose flour
1 tbs. granulated sugar
2 tsp. baking powder
1 tsp. salt
1/2 tsp. baking soda
1 cup sour cream
2 eggs
4 tbs. unsalted butter, melted
1 cup cooked whole kernel corn
4 green onions, thinly sliced
4 oz. can diced green chiles, drained
1/2 cup whole milk, if needed

Preheat the oven to 425°. Spray a 12 cup muffin tin with non stick cooking spray. Place the muffin tin in the oven for 2 minutes to get hot before you add the batter.

In a mixing bowl, add the blue cornmeal, all purpose flour, granulated sugar, baking powder, salt and baking soda. Stir until well combined.

In a separate bowl, add the sour cream, eggs, butter, corn, green onions and green chiles. Stir until well combined. Add this mixture to the dry ingredients. Mix only until well combined. Every cornmeal is different and absorbs liquids differently. Add milk as needed to make a batter similar to a consistency of thick cake batter.

Spoon the batter into the hot muffin tin filling the muffin cups about 2/3 full. Bake for 14-18 minutes or until the muffins are firm and browned. Remove the pan from the oven and let the muffins rest for 5 minutes before serving.

Serving suggestion: Spread with butter or serve with any main dish or casserole. Very good with soups and chili.

Vegetable Muffins

Makes 12 muffins

1/2 cup fresh zucchini, finely chopped
1/2 cup carrots, grated
1 cup whole wheat flour
1 cup all purpose flour
1 tbs. baking powder
1/2 cup granulated sugar
1/4 cup raisins
2 eggs
1 cup whole milk
6 tbs. vegetable oil

Preheat the oven to 350°. Spray a 12 cup muffin tin with non stick cooking spray. In a mixing bowl, add the zucchini, carrots, whole wheat flour, all purpose flour, baking powder, granulated sugar and raisins. Stir until well blended.

Add the eggs, milk and vegetable oil. Mix only until the batter is combined and moistened. Spoon the batter into the prepared muffin tin filling the muffin cups about 2/3 full. Bake for 16-18 minutes or until the muffins are firm to the touch and golden brown. Remove the muffins from the oven and let the muffins cool for 5 minutes before removing them from the pan.

Serving suggestion: Serve with any meat or casserole dish. Especially good with beans or beef stew. Serve with a deli meat and cheese platter along with fresh fruit for a fast meal in the summertime.

Note: You can reduce the granulated sugar to 1/4 cup if desired.

Cheddar Cheese Black Pepper Muffins

Makes 12 muffins

1 1/2 cups all purpose flour
1 tbs. baking powder
1/4 tsp. salt
1 tsp. coarse ground black pepper
1 tsp. dry mustard
3/4 cup shredded sharp cheddar cheese
1 tsp. granulated sugar
1/4 cup vegetable oil
1 egg
1/3 to 1/2 cup whole milk
1/3 cup water

Preheat the oven to 350°. Spray a 12 cup muffin tin with non stick cooking spray. In a mixing bowl, add the all purpose flour, baking powder, salt, black pepper, mustard, cheddar cheese and granulated sugar. Stir until well combined.

In a separate bowl, add the vegetable oil, egg, 1/3 cup milk and water. Whisk until well blended. Pour the mixture into the dry ingredients. Mix only until the batter is moistened and combined. Add the remaining milk if needed to make a moist batter.

Pour the batter into the prepared muffin tin filling the muffin cups about 2/3 full. Bake for 16-20 minutes or until the muffins are firm to the touch and golden brown. Let the muffins rest for 5 minutes in the pan before removing the muffins.

Serving suggestion: Serve for breakfast with eggs, bacon or sausage. The muffin is a great replacement for dinner rolls. Serve with any meat or casserole.

Italian Cornbread Muffins

Makes 12 muffins

2 large eggs
1 cup whole milk
1/4 cup vegetable oil or melted lard
1 1/2 cups plain yellow cornmeal
1 cup all purpose flour
2 tbs. granulated sugar
3/4 tsp. salt
1 tbs. dried Italian Seasoning
3 tbs. minced garlic (fresh or dried)
1 cup shredded cheddar cheese or fresh Parmesan cheese
3 tbs. melted unsalted butter
1 tbs. minced garlic
Vegetable oil or garlic oil for greasing muffin pan

Make the garlic butter by combining 3 tablespoons melted butter and 1 tablespoon of minced garlic in a small bowl. Stir to combine and let the butter sit for 10 minutes. The butter may harden a little but that is alright.

In a mixing bowl, combine all of the remaining ingredients except for the oil for your pan. Stir only until the batter is combined and moistened. Let the batter sit for 3 minutes. Preheat your oven to 450°.

Grease a 12 cup muffin tin vegetable oil or garlic oil. Don't skimp on greasing the pan or the muffins will stick. Place the muffin tin in the oven for a few minutes to heat. Divide the cornmeal batter between the muffin cups and bake about 15-20 minutes or until they are done in the center and lightly browned. Brush with garlic butter and serve hot. Split open the cornbread muffins and spread with additional garlic butter if desired. So good!

Serving suggestion: Use instead of garlic bread for any Italian meal. Delicious with soups and salads.

2 QUICK BREADS

Bacon Egg & Cheese Spoon Bread

Makes 8 servings

3/4 cup yellow or white plain cornmeal
1 1/2 cups cold water
2 cups grated cheddar cheese
1/4 cup unsalted butter, softened
2 cloves minced garlic
1/2 tsp. salt
1 cup whole milk
6 egg yolks, well beaten
10 slices cooked and crumbled bacon
6 egg whites, stiffly beaten

Preheat the oven to 325°. In a large sauce pan over medium heat, add the cornmeal and the water. Bring the water to a boil and stir until the cornmeal is thick as mush or about 3-4 minutes. Remove the pan from the heat and add the cheddar cheese, butter, garlic and salt. Stir to melt the cheese. Gradually add the milk and the egg yolks, mixing well. Add about 2/3 of the crumbled bacon and stir gently. Fold in the egg whites and pour the batter into a greased 3 quart baking dish. Bake for one hour or until the spoon bread is golden brown. Top the bread with the remaining bacon crumbles and serve.

Serving suggestion: Use as a side dish and serve with any meat or casserole dish.

Chili Pepper Parmesan Spoon Bread

Makes 6 servings

1 cup self rising white cornmeal
2 cups water
2 tbs. unsalted butter
1 tsp. granulated sugar
1/3 cup grated Parmesan cheese
1 cup whole milk
1/4 cup chopped roasted chili peppers
3 eggs, separated

In a mixing bowl, add the egg whites. Beat the egg whites with a mixer on medium speed until stiff peaks form. Set the egg whites aside for the moment.

Preheat the oven to 375°. Spray a deep 2 quart casserole dish with non stick cooking spray. In a sauce pan over medium low heat, add the water. When the water starts to boil, add the cornmeal. Stir constantly until the cornmeal dissolves and begins to thicken. This should take a couple of minutes.

Remove the pan from the heat and add the butter, granulated sugar, Parmesan cheese, milk, egg yolks and chili peppers. Stir until well combined. Gently fold the beaten egg whites into the cornmeal. Spoon the batter into the prepared dish. Bake for 45-55 minutes or until the spoon bread is set in the center. Remove the pan from the oven and serve immediately.

Serving suggestion: Delicious with most any main dish or casserole. Use the spoon bread as a side dish or in place of rolls or other dinner breads. Seasoned taco meat or fajitas are delicious spooned over servings of the spoon bread.

Southern Hush Puppies

Makes about 20 hush puppies

1 cup plain white corn meal
1 clove crushed garlic
2 tbs. finely chopped onion
1/2 tsp. salt
2 tbs. baking powder
2 tbs. all purpose flour
2 eggs
1/4 cup whole milk
Vegetable oil for frying

In a mixing bowl, combine all the ingredients except the vegetable oil. Mix until the batter is combined.

Preheat the oil in a pot to 365°. The oil needs to be at least 2" deep in your pot. Drop the batter by teaspoonfuls into the hot oil. Fry on each side about 2 minutes or until the hush puppies are done and golden brown.

Note: Hush puppies can be hard to tell when they are done in the center. I usually cook one for 1-2 minutes on each side and then break it open. If it looks done, I cook the rest this way or add a minute or two cooking time. Don't make the hush puppy too large.

When I am in a hurry, I cook these in a skillet. Place about 1/8 cup vegetable oil in your skillet and cook over medium high heat. Place about 1/4 cup batter in the skillet and cook the hush puppies like pancakes. Repeat adding more oil if necessary until all the batter is used.

Serving suggestion: Great with any meal or by themselves. Delicious with fried catfish and coleslaw.

Sweet Potato Hush Puppies

Makes about 16 hush puppies

Vegetable oil for frying
1 cup cooked sweet potatoes
4 eggs
1/2 cup yellow or white plain cornmeal
1/2 cup all purpose flour
1/2 tsp. salt
1/2 tsp. ground cinnamon
1/4 tsp. black pepper
4 tbs. chopped onion

Preheat the vegetable oil in a deep fryer or deep sauce pan to 350°. The oil needs to be about 3" deep in the pan.

In a mixing bowl, add the sweet potatoes and eggs. Whisk until well combined. Add the cornmeal, all purpose flour, salt, ground cinnamon, black pepper and onion. Mix only until combined. Drop the batter by tablespoonfuls into the hot oil. Fry for 2-3 minutes or until golden brown.

The outside should be golden brown and the inside soft and moist.

Note: Hush puppies can be hard to tell when they are done in the center. I usually cook one for 1-2 minutes on each side and then break it open. If it looks done, I cook the rest this way or add a minute or two cooking time. Don't make the hush puppy too large.

Serving suggestion: Serve with any meat or casserole. They are delicious with soups and stews.

Beer Batter Hush Puppies

Makes 16 hush puppies

Vegetable oil for frying
1 cup yellow or white plain cornmeal
3/4 cup all purpose flour
2 tsp. baking powder
3/4 tsp. salt
1 tbs. granulated sugar
1/2 cup finely chopped onion
2 green onions, chopped
1 egg
1/2 cup beer
4 drops Tabasco sauce

Preheat the vegetable oil in a deep fryer or deep sauce pan to 360°. The oil needs to be at least 2" deep in the pot.

In a mixing bowl, add the cornmeal, all purpose flour, baking powder, salt, granulated sugar, onion and green onions. Stir until well combined. Add the egg, beer and Tabasco sauce. Stir until the batter is well combined.

Add additional beer if needed to make a batter that is thick enough to be dropped from a spoon but thin enough to cook well. It is a thin line when using cornmeal as each cornmeal absorbs liquids differently.

Drop the batter by teaspoonfuls into the hot oil. Cook the hush puppies for 1-2 minutes per side. They should be golden brown and floating on top of the oil when ready.

Serving suggestion: Serve in place of dinner rolls with most any meal. Delicious with chili and hearty stews.

Parmesan Herb Quick Bread

Makes 1 loaf

2 onions, chopped
3 tbs. vegetable oil
3/4 cup sour cream
1/2 cup vegetable oil
2 eggs
1 3/4 cups all purpose flour
1/2 cup freshly grated Parmesan cheese
1 tbs. granulated sugar
2 tsp. fresh minced rosemary
2 tsp. fresh minced thyme
1 1/2 tsp. baking powder
1 tsp. lemon zest
1/2 tsp. salt
1/2 tsp. black pepper
1/4 tsp. baking soda

Preheat the oven to 350°. Spray a loaf pan with non stick cooking spray. In a skillet over medium low heat, add the onions and 3 tablespoons vegetable oil. Stir frequently and saute the onions for 8-12 minutes. The onions should be caramelized.

Remove the onions from the heat and add the sour cream, 1/2 cup vegetable oil and eggs. Whisk until well combined.

In a mixing bowl, add the all purpose flour, Parmesan cheese, granulated sugar, rosemary, thyme, baking powder, lemon zest, salt, black pepper and baking soda. Stir until well combined. Add the onion mixture and mix only until combined and moistened.

Spoon the batter into the prepared pan. Bake for 40-50 minutes or until the center of the bread test clean with a toothpick. Remove the bread from the oven and cool the bread for 10 minutes in the pan. Cool the bread completely before slicing.

Serving suggestion: Serve the bread toasted with butter, cheese spread or as is with any meat or casserole. Great bread to use for sandwiches.

Quick Herb Batter Bread

Makes 1 loaf

3 cups all purpose flour
2 tbs. granulated sugar
1 tbs. baking powder
2 tsp. caraway seeds
1/2 tsp. salt
1/2 tsp. dried thyme
1/2 tsp. ground nutmeg
1 egg, beaten
1 1/2 cups whole milk
1/2 cup vegetable oil

Preheat the oven to 350°. In a large mixing bowl, add the all purpose flour, granulated sugar, baking powder, caraway seeds, salt, thyme and nutmeg. Stir until well combined. In a separate mixing bowl, mix together the egg, milk and vegetable oil. Add the wet ingredients to the flour ingredients. Stir to form the batter. Do not over mix as this will make the bread tough.

Spray an 8" loaf pan with non stick cooking spray. Pour the batter into the loaf pan and bake for 50-55 minutes or until a toothpick inserted in the center of the bread comes out clean. Remove the bread from the oven and cool the bread for 15 minutes in the pan. Cool the bread completely before slicing.

Note: You can use any spice combination instead of the caraway seeds, thyme and nutmeg listed above. Use 3 teaspoons of your favorite herb combination for different flavors.

Serving suggestion: Use the bread for sandwiches or burgers. Toast the bread and serve with butter. The bread goes well with Italian dishes and most casseroles.

Fresh Dill Beer Bread

Makes one loaf

3 cups self rising flour
3 tbs. light brown sugar
1 tbs. fresh dill
12 oz. can light beer
2 tbs. melted butter

Preheat the oven to 375°. Grease a 9" loaf pan with non stick cooking spray. In a mixing bowl, add the self rising flour, dill, brown sugar and beer. Using a mixer on medium speed, beat the batter until well combined. Pour the batter into the prepared loaf pan. Pour the melted butter over the batter. Bake for 45-50 minutes or until the bread test done in the center.

Remove the bread from the oven and cool the bread in the pan for 15 minutes before removing the bread from the pan. Cool completely before slicing.

Serving suggestion: This is very good with fried ham and eggs. Try this bread with sandwiches and hamburgers instead of buns.

Beer Bread

Makes 1 loaf

3 cups self rising flour
1/2 cup granulated sugar
12 oz. beer
2 tbs. unsalted butter, melted

Preheat the oven to 350°. In a mixing bowl, add the self rising flour, granulated sugar and beer. Mix only until well combined and moistened. Pour the batter into the prepared pan. Bake for 35-45 minutes. The bread should almost be done. Pour the melted butter over the bread. Bake for 10-15 minutes or until the bread is done and golden brown.

Remove the bread from the oven and cool the bread in the pan for 15 minutes. Remove the bread from the pan and cool completely before slicing.

Serving suggestion: Use this bread for sandwiches, croutons, cut into cubes for fondue or serve with any meal.

Bacon, Onion & Kale Bread

Makes 1 loaf

2 purple onions, chopped
2 tbs. olive oil
5 oz. kale
3/4 cup sour cream
2 eggs
1/2 cup vegetable oil
1 3/4 cups all purpose flour
1 tbs. granulated sugar
1 1/2 tsp. baking powder
1 tsp. lemon zest
1/2 tsp. salt
1/2 tsp. black pepper
1/4 tsp. baking soda
1/2 cup crumbled & cooked bacon
1/4 tsp. cayenne pepper

Preheat the oven to 350°. Spray a loaf pan with non stick cooking spray. In a skillet over medium low heat, add the olive oil and onions. Saute the onions for 10 minutes. Add the kale and saute the kale for 8 minutes. Remove the skillet from the heat and add the sour cream, eggs and vegetable oil. Whisk until well combined.

In a mixing bowl, add the all purpose flour, granulated sugar, baking powder, lemon zest, salt, black pepper, baking soda, bacon and cayenne pepper. Stir until well combined. Add the onions and kale mixture from the skillet. Stir only until the ingredients are moistened and combined.

Pour the batter into the prepared loaf pan. Bake for 40-50 minutes or until the center of the bread test done with a toothpick. Remove the bread from the oven and cool for 10 minutes in the pan. Cool completely before slicing.

Serving suggestion: Toast the bread and spread with your favorite cheese, make sandwiches with the bread or serve with any meal instead of rolls.

Bacon Cheese Bread

Makes 1 loaf

3 tbs. unsalted butter
2 onions, chopped
10 slices bacon
2 cups all purpose flour
1 tbs. baking powder
2 tsp. salt
1/2 tsp. black pepper
1 cup whole milk
1/3 cup vegetable oil
1 egg
2 cups sharp cheddar cheese, shredded

Preheat the oven to 350°. Spray a loaf pan with non stick cooking spray. In a skillet over medium low heat, add the butter and onions. Saute the onions for 12-15 minutes. Stir frequently to keep the onions from burning. The onions should be golden brown when ready. Remove the skillet from the heat.

In a separate skillet, add the bacon. Cook the bacon over medium low heat until the bacon is done and crispy. Remove the bacon from the skillet and drain on paper towels. Crumble the bacon into small pieces.

Add the milk, vegetable oil and the egg to the skillet with the onions. Mix until well combined. In a mixing bowl, add the all purpose flour, baking powder, salt, black pepper, cheese and bacon. Stir until combined. Add the ingredients from the skillet with the onions and mix only until the batter is moistened and combined.

Pour the batter into the prepared pan. Bake for 35-50 minutes or until the bread test done in the center with a toothpick. Cool the bread in pan for 15 minutes before removing the bread from the pan.

Serving suggestion: This bread makes an excellent egg sandwich and is delicious by itself or served with any meal.

Green Chile Cheese Popcorn Bread

Makes 1 loaf

4 cups popped popcorn
3 tbs. vegetable oil
1 cup plain yellow cornmeal
2 tbs. granulated sugar
2 tsp. baking powder
1/2 tsp. salt
1 egg
1 cup whole milk
1/4 cup vegetable oil
1 cup shredded Pepper Jack cheese
4 oz. can diced green chiles, drained

Preheat the oven to 400°. Place the vegetable oil in an 8" cast iron skillet. Place the skillet in the oven and heat until the oil is sizzling hot. In a food processor, add the popcorn and blend until the popcorn is well ground. Add the cornmeal, granulated sugar, baking powder and salt. Blend until well combined.

In a mixing bowl, add the egg, milk, vegetable oil, 3/4 cup cheese and green chiles. Stir until combined. Add the dry ingredients from the blender. Stir only until the batter is moistened. Pour the batter into the hot skillet. Sprinkle the remaining 1/4 cup Pepper Jack cheese over the top of the batter. Bake for 20-25 minutes or until the bread test done in the center with a toothpick and is golden brown. Invert the skillet onto a platter and serve hot.

Serving suggestion: This bread is excellent with soups, stews and casseroles.

Dill Pickle Bread

Makes 1 loaf

2 onions, chopped
3 tbs. vegetable oil
3/4 cup plain Greek yogurt
1/2 cup vegetable oil
2 eggs
1 3/4 cups all purpose flour
1 tbs. granulated sugar
1 1/2 tsp. baking powder
1/2 tsp. salt
1/2 tsp. black pepper
1/4 tsp. baking soda
1/4 cup chopped fresh dill
2 tsp. dill seeds
1/4 cup chopped dill pickle
1 tbs. pickle juice

Preheat the oven to 350°. Spray a loaf pan with non stick cooking spray. In a skillet over medium low heat, add 3 tablespoons vegetable oil and the onions. Stir frequently and saute the onions for 12 minutes. The onions should be golden brown. Remove the pan from the heat and add the yogurt, 1/2 cup vegetable oil, pickle juice and eggs. Whisk until well combined.

In a mixing bowl, add the all purpose flour, granulated sugar, baking powder, salt, black pepper, baking soda, fresh dill, dill seeds and dill pickle. Stir until combined. Add the ingredients from the skillet and mix only until the batter is moistened. Spoon the batter into the prepared pan.

Bake for 40-55 minutes or until the center of the bread test done with a toothpick. Remove the bread from the oven and cool the bread for 15 minutes in the pan. Remove the bread from the pan and cool completely before slicing.

Serving suggestion: Use as a bread for sandwiches or spread with goat cheese or cream cheese.

Cheddar Squash Bread

Makes 1 loaf

1/4 cup vegetable oil
2 cups all purpose flour
1/4 cup plain yellow cornmeal
2 tsp. baking powder
1 1/4 tsp. dried oregano
3/4 tsp. salt
1/2 tsp. baking soda
1/2 tsp. black pepper
2 eggs
3/4 cup whole milk
2 cups grated yellow squash
2/3 cup crumbled sharp cheddar cheese

Drain all water from the grated squash. Preheat the oven to 350°. Spray a loaf pan with non stick cooking spray. In a mixing bowl, add the all purpose flour, cornmeal, baking powder, oregano, salt, baking soda, black pepper and cheese. Mix until combined.

In a separate bowl, add the vegetable oil, eggs, milk and squash. Stir until combined. Add the dry ingredients and mix only until the batter is moistened. Pour the batter into the prepared pan. Bake for 50-60 minutes or until the center of the bread test clean with a toothpick. Remove the bread from the oven and cool for 15 minutes before removing the bread from the pan.

You can slice this bread warm but it tends to crumble. I cool the bread completely and then toast the slices to warm them up.

Serving suggestion: Serve with beans, fresh tomatoes and greens for a delicious supper. Spread the bread with butter and serve. Delicious with hearty stews and chili.

Ham & Cheese Olive Loaf

Makes 1 loaf

2 1/2 cups all purpose flour
2 1/4 tsp. baking powder
1/2 tsp. salt
1/4 tsp. baking soda
1//4 tsp. black pepper
1 1/2 cups shredded cheddar, Pepper Jack or Monterey cheese
1 1/4 cups cooked ham, diced
1/3 cup black olives, diced
2 eggs
3/4 cup whole milk
4 tbs. unsalted butter, melted

Preheat the oven to 350°. Spray a loaf pan with non stick cooking spray. In a mixing bowl, add the all purpose flour, baking powder, salt, baking soda, black pepper, cheese, ham and olives. Stir until well combined.

In a separate bowl, add the eggs, milk and melted butter. Stir until well blended. Add the wet ingredients to the dry ingredients and mix only until the batter is moistened. Pour the batter into the prepared pan. Bake for 40-45 minutes or until the center of the bread test done with a toothpick.

Remove the bread from the oven and cool the bread in the pan for 15 minutes. Cool the bread for 30 minutes before slicing.

Serving suggestion: Serve toasted for breakfast with fried eggs or spread with cream cheese. Goes well with most any salad or soup.

Tabasco Onion Cheese Bread

Makes 1 loaf

2 onions, chopped
2 tbs. vegetable oil
3/4 cup sour cream
1/2 cup vegetable oil
2 eggs
1 3/4 cups all purpose flour
1 tbs. granulated sugar
1 1/2 tsp. baking powder
1/2 tsp. salt
1/2 tsp. black pepper
1/4 tsp. baking soda
1 tsp. paprika
1/2 tsp. celery seeds
1 cup shredded Monterey Jack cheese
2 tbs. Tabasco sauce

Preheat the oven to 350°. Spray a loaf pan with non stick cooking spray. In a skillet over medium low heat, add the onions and 2 tablespoons vegetable oil. Saute the onions for 10 minutes. The onions should be golden brown. Remove the skillet from the heat.

Add the sour cream, 1/2 cup vegetable oil, eggs and Tabasco sauce to the onions. Stir until well blended.

In a mixing bowl, add the all purpose flour, granulated sugar, baking powder, salt, black pepper, baking soda, paprika, celery seeds and 3/4 cup cheese. Stir until combined. Add the onion and all ingredients from the skillet. Mix only until the batter is moistened. Pour the batter into the prepared pan. Sprinkle the remaining cheese over the top of the batter. Bake for 40-50 minutes or until a toothpick inserted in the center of the bread comes out clean. Remove the bread from the oven and cool the bread for 15 minutes in the pan. Cool the bread for an additional 15 minutes before slicing.

Spinach Garlic Quick Bread

Makes 1 loaf

1 tbs. vegetable oil
1 onion, thinly sliced
1 tsp. salt
2 cups fresh spinach leaves
2 garlic cloves, minced
2 1/2 cups all purpose flour
2 tsp. baking powder
2 eggs, beaten
3/4 cup whole milk
2/3 cup vegetable oil

Preheat the oven to 350°. Spray a loaf pan with non stick cooking spray. Stir frequently while cooking the vegetables. In a skillet over medium low heat, add 1 tablespoon vegetable oil, 1/2 teaspoon salt and the onion. Saute the onion for 7-8 minutes or until the onion is golden brown. Add the garlic and cook for 1 minute. Add the spinach leaves and cook for 2 minutes. Remove the pan from the heat and stir in the milk, 2/3 cup vegetable oil and eggs.

In a mixing bowl, add the all purpose flour, 1/2 teaspoon salt and the baking powder. Stir until well blended. Add the ingredients from the skillet and mix only until the batter is moistened.

Spoon the batter into the prepared pan. Bake for 35-40 minutes or until the center of the bread test done with a toothpick and the bread is golden brown. Remove the bread from the oven and cool for 15 minutes in the pan. Cool the bread before slicing.

Serving suggestion: Serve with soups or salads. This bread goes well with most any casserole or use in place of garlic bread.

Green Onion Bread

Makes 1 loaf

2 cups all purpose flour
2 tsp. baking powder
1 tsp. granulated sugar
1/2 tsp. baking soda
1/2 tsp. salt
1 cup sliced green onions
3/4 cup whole milk
2 tsp. vinegar
3 tbs. unsalted butter, melted
1 egg
1/4 cup grated Parmesan cheese

Preheat the oven to 350°. Spray a loaf pan with non stick cooking spray. In a mixing bowl, add the all purpose flour, baking powder, granulated sugar, baking soda, salt, Parmesan cheese and green onions. Stir until combined.

In a separate bowl, add the milk, vinegar, egg and melted butter. Whisk until well combined. Add the wet ingredients to the dry ingredients and mix only until the batter is moistened.

Place the dough on a lightly floured surface. Knead the dough 5-6 times. Flatten the dough with your hand and place in the prepared pan. Flatten the dough to fit the pan if needed. Bake for 30-40 minutes or until the bread test done in the center with a toothpick and is golden brown. Remove the bread from the oven and cool the bread for 15 minutes in the pan. Cool completely before slicing.

Serving suggestion: Use in place of bread or buns for sandwiches. Serve toasted with chive cream cheese or cut into bite size pieces for croutons. Excellent with soups and stews.

Olive Quick Bread

Makes 1 loaf

3/4 cup sour cream
1/2 cup olive oil
2 eggs
1 3/4 cups all purpose flour
1/2 cup freshly grated Parmesan cheese
1 tbs. granulated sugar
2 tsp. fresh chopped rosemary
1 1/2 tsp. baking powder
1 tsp. fresh lemon zest
1/2 tsp. salt
1/2 tsp. black pepper
1/4 tsp. baking soda
1 cup diced green or black olives

Preheat the oven to 350°. Spray a loaf pan with non stick cooking spray. In a mixing bowl, add the all purpose flour, Parmesan cheese, sugar, rosemary, baking powder, lemon zest, salt, black pepper, baking soda and green olives. Stir until combined.

In a separate bowl, add the sour cream, olive oil and eggs. Whisk until well combined. Pour the mixture into the dry ingredients. Mix only until the batter is moistened. Spoon the batter into the prepared pan. Bake for 35-50 minutes or until the bread test done in the center with a toothpick and is golden brown.

Remove the bread from the oven and let the bread cool for 15 minutes in the pan. Cool completely before slicing.

Serving suggestion: Spread with your favorite cheese spread, use as a base for individual pizzas, great with soups and salads.

Black Pepper Cheddar Bread

Makes 1 loaf

2 cups bread flour
1 cup shredded sharp cheddar cheese
1 tsp. granulated sugar
1/2 tsp. baking powder
1/2 tsp. baking soda
1/2 tsp. salt
1 1/2 tsp. black pepper
1 cup whole milk
1/3 cup unsalted butter, melted
2 eggs

Preheat the oven to 350°. Spray a loaf pan with non stick cooking spray. In a mixing bowl, add the bread flour, cheese, sugar, baking powder, baking soda, salt and black pepper. Stir until well combined.

In a separate bowl, add the milk, butter and eggs. Whisk until well blended. Add the milk mixture to the dry ingredients. Mix only until the batter is moistened. Spoon the batter into the prepared pan. Bake for 35-45 minutes or until the center of the bread test done with a toothpick and is golden brown.

Remove the pan from the oven and cool the bread for 15 minutes in the pan. Cool the bread completely before slicing. Store the bread in the refrigerator.

Serving suggestion: Serve in place of rolls for dinner. The bread goes well with casseroles, soups and stews. Use bread slices for sandwiches and burgers.

Green Bell Pepper Quick Bread

Makes 1 loaf

2 eggs
1/4 cup unsalted butter, melted
1 cup whole milk
1/2 cup green bell pepper, minced
1/4 cup Parmesan cheese
1 tsp. dried basil
1/4 tsp. dried rosemary
2 cups all purpose flour
1 1/2 tsp. baking powder
1/2 tsp. baking soda
1/2 tsp. salt
1/4 tsp. black pepper

Preheat the oven to 350°. Spray a loaf pan with non stick cooking spray. In a mixing bowl, add the green bell pepper, Parmesan cheese, basil, rosemary, all purpose flour, baking powder, baking soda, salt and black pepper. Stir until well combined.

In a separate bowl, add the eggs, butter and whole milk. Whisk until well combined. Pour the egg mixture into the dry ingredients. Mix only until the batter is moistened. Pour the batter into the prepared pan. Bake for 40-50 minutes or until the center of the bread test done with a toothpick.

Remove the bread from the oven and cool the bread in the pan for 15 minutes. Cool completely before slicing.

Serving suggestion: Spread the bread with garlic butter to use in place of garlic bread. Makes wonderful bread for sandwiches. Use slices of the bread as a base for pizza or tacos.

Tomato Cilantro Quick Bread

Makes 1 loaf

2 cups all purpose flour
1 tsp. baking soda
1 tbs. baking powder
1 tsp. salt
1 tsp. ground cumin
1/2 cup fresh cilantro
3 green onions, sliced
3 medium tomatoes, seeded and diced
1 roasted jalapeno pepper, chopped
1 tbs. tomato paste
3/4 cup granulated sugar
3 eggs

You need about 2 1/4 cups diced tomatoes. More than that will make the bread soupy. If your tomatoes are juicy, use about 1 1/4 cups tomatoes. If the batter is too dry, you can puree the remaining tomatoes and add to the batter.

Warning: You need to lean on the side of caution with the tomato puree. Too much juice and your bread is destroyed. Add 1 1/4 cups and then add the remaining as needed. Every tomato purees differently so be prepared.

Preheat the oven to 350°. Spray a loaf pan with non stick cooking spray. In a food processor, add the cilantro, green onions, tomatoes, jalapeno pepper and granulated sugar. Process until well combined.

Pour the mixture from the food processor into a mixing bowl. Add the eggs and tomato paste. Stir until well combined. Add the all purpose flour, baking soda, baking powder, salt and ground cumin. Mix only until the batter is moistened. Spoon the batter into the prepared pan. Bake for 40-45 minutes or until the bread test done in the center with a toothpick and is golden brown. Remove the bread from the oven and cool the bread for 15 minutes in the pan.

Savory Swiss Olive Bread

Makes 1 loaf

2 cups self rising flour
1/4 tsp. garlic powder
3/4 cup whole milk
1/2 cup unsalted butter, melted
2 eggs
1 1/2 cups shredded Swiss cheese
3/4 cup sliced Kalamata olives
2 tbs. fresh chopped basil

Preheat the oven to 350°. Spray a loaf pan with non stick cooking spray. In a mixing bowl, add the self rising flour, garlic powder, basil, Swiss cheese and olives. Toss until well combined.

In a separate bowl, add the melted butter, eggs and milk. Whisk until well combined. Add the egg and milk mixture to the dry ingredients. Mix only until the batter is moistened and combined.

Pour the batter into the prepared pan. Bake for 45-55 minutes or until the bread test done with a toothpick in the center. Remove the bread from the oven and cool the bread for 10 minutes before removing the bread from the pan. Cool the bread completely before slicing.

Serving suggestion: This bread makes excellent sandwiches. Toast the bread and pile on your favorite sandwich fixings. This is a good bread to make when you run out of sandwich bread.

Sage Cornbread

Makes an 8" skillet

2 tbs. vegetable oil
3/4 cup plain yellow cornmeal
1 cup all purpose flour
1 tbs. granulated sugar
1 tbs. baking powder
1/2 tsp. salt
1 tbs. fresh sage, minced
1 cup whole milk
1 egg
2 tbs. unsalted butter, melted

Preheat the oven to 425°. Place the vegetable oil in an 8" cast iron skillet. Heat the skillet in the oven for 2-3 minutes before adding the batter.

In a mixing bowl, add the cornmeal, all purpose flour, granulated sugar, baking powder, salt and sage. Stir until well combined. Add the egg, milk and butter. Mix only until the batter is well combined.

Pour the batter into the hot skillet. Bake for 18-25 minutes or until the cornbread is done and golden brown.

Serving suggestion: Serve with any soup, stew or chili. This cornbread makes excellent dressing or stuffing. Spread the cornbread with butter and serve with any main dish or casserole. Very good with chicken dishes.

Salsa Cornbread

Makes a 9" skillet

3 tbs. vegetable oil
1 1/2 cups white or yellow self rising cornmeal
1/2 tsp. garlic powder
1 egg
1/2 cup whole milk
1/2 cup salsa
4 oz. can diced green chiles, drained

Preheat the oven to 425°. Add 2 tablespoons vegetable oil to a 9" cast iron skillet. Heat the skillet and oil for 3-4 minutes before adding the batter.

In a mixing bowl, add the egg, 1 tablespoon vegetable oil, milk, salsa and green chiles. Whisk until well combined. Add the cornmeal and garlic powder. Stir until the batter is moistened and combined.

Pour the batter into the hot skillet. Bake for 20-25 minutes or until the cornbread is firm, golden brown and the crust is crispy. Remove the cornbread from the oven and serve hot.

Serving suggestion: This cornbread goes well with beans, greens, soups, stews, chili or salads. Use the cornbread in place of taco shells for super delicious tacos or burritos.

Onion Cornbread

Makes a 9" skillet

2 tbs. vegetable oil
2 cups self rising yellow or white cornmeal
1 onion, chopped
1/2 cup vegetable oil
1 cup sour cream
2 eggs
1 cup cream style corn
1/2 cup whole milk, if needed

Preheat the oven to 425°. Place 2 tablespoons vegetable oil in a 9" cast iron skillet. Heat the skillet for 2-3 minutes before adding the batter.

In a mixing bowl, add 1/2 cup vegetable oil, sour cream, eggs and corn. Stir until well combined. Add the cornmeal and onion. Stir until the batter is combined.

Every cornmeal absorbs liquids differently. Add milk if needed to make the batter the consistency of cake batter. Pour the batter into the pan and bake for 30-35 minutes or until the cornbread is done and golden brown. Remove the skillet from the oven and serve hot.

Serving suggestion: This goes well with most any meal. Delicious with soups or salads. Spread butter over the top for extra good eating!

Butternut Squash Cornbread

Makes an 8" skillet

1 cup plain yellow or white cornmeal
1 cup all purpose flour
1 tsp. baking soda
1 1/2 tsp. baking powder
1/2 tsp. salt
1 tbs. to 1/4 cup light brown sugar
1 egg
1/2 to 3/4 cup whole milk
1 cup cooked butternut squash, mashed
7 tsp. vegetable oil

Preheat the oven to 400°. Add 4 teaspoons vegetable oil to a 9" cast iron skillet. Heat the skillet in the oven for 2-3 minutes before adding the batter.

If you like your cornbread a little sweet, add 1/4 cup brown sugar. I like my cornbread less sweet so I only use 1 tablespoon brown sugar.

In a mixing bowl, add the cornmeal, all purpose flour, baking soda, baking powder, salt and brown sugar. Stir until well combined. Add the egg, 1/2 cup milk, squash and 3 teaspoons vegetable oil. Stir until well combined. Add the remaining milk if needed to make a thick but pourable batter.

Add the batter to the hot skillet. Bake for 25-30 minutes or until the cornbread is done and golden brown. Remove the skillet from the oven and invert the cornbread onto a serving plate.

Serving suggestion: Serve with plenty of butter and maple syrup if desired. Very good with stews and soups. I like to serve this cornbread alongside large main dish salads with iced tea.

Cheddar Bacon Cornbread

Makes a 10" skillet

1/4 cup vegetable oil
2 tbs. bacon drippings
5 slices bacon, cooked and crumbled
1 1/2 cups plain yellow or white cornmeal
1/2 cup all purpose flour
1 tsp. salt
2 tsp. baking powder
1 cup sharp cheddar cheese, shredded
2 eggs
1 1/2 cups whole milk

Preheat the oven to 400°. Place the bacon drippings in a 10" cast iron skillet. Heat the skillet for 2-3 minutes before adding the batter.

In a mixing bowl, add the cornmeal, all purpose flour, bacon, salt, baking powder and cheddar cheese. Stir until combined. Add the vegetable oil, eggs and milk. Mix until well combined. Pour the batter into the hot skillet.

Bake for 20-25 minutes or until the cornbread is done and golden brown. Remove the skillet from the oven and invert the cornbread onto a serving plate.

Serving suggestion: Delicious with butter or sorghum. Serve alongside any soup or stew. Goes well with any main dish or casserole.

Southern Breakfast Cornbread

Makes a 9 x 13 pan

2 tbs. unsalted butter
4 tbs. unsalted butter, melted
1 lb. pork sausage, cooked and crumbled
2 cups plain yellow or white cornmeal
3/4 cup all purpose flour
1 tbs. baking powder
1 1/2 tsp. baking soda
1/2 tsp. salt
2 eggs, beaten
2 cups whole milk
Maple syrup or sorghum, optional

Preheat the oven to 400°. Place 2 tablespoons butter in a 9 x 13 pan. Place the pan in the oven for 2-3 minutes before adding the batter. The butter should be melted and sizzling hot before adding the batter.

In a mixing bowl, add 4 tablespoons melted butter, sausage, eggs and milk. Whisk until well combined. Add the cornmeal, all purpose flour, baking powder, baking soda and salt. Stir the batter until well combined. Spoon the batter into the hot pan. Bake for 20-25 minutes or until the cornbread is set and done. Remove the cornbread from the oven and cut into squares. Serve with maple syrup or sorghum over the top.

Note: 1 pound of diced cooked ham or bacon can be used instead of the sausage. I have used a combination of sausage, ham and bacon for a different flavor that is delicious. This can be made the night before and refrigerated until ready to bake. Add 10-20 minutes additional cooking time if made ahead.

Serving suggestion: Use as a main dish for dinner. Make the bread in the morning and all you have to do is cook the bread when you get home.

Broccoli Cornbread

Makes a 9" cast iron skillet

1/4 cup plus 2 tbs. vegetable oil
1 1/4 cups whole milk
2 eggs
2 cups white or yellow self rising cornmeal
1/4 tsp. onion powder
1/4 tsp. black pepper
1 1/2 cups shredded cheddar cheese
2 cups frozen broccoli, thawed and finely cut

Preheat the oven to 425°. Add 2 tablespoons vegetable oil to a 9" cast iron skillet. Heat the skillet and the oil for 3-4 minutes before adding the batter.

In a mixing bowl, add 1/4 cup vegetable oil, milk and eggs. Whisk until well blended. Add the cornmeal, onion powder, black pepper, cheese and broccoli. Stir only until the batter is well combined.

Pour the batter into the hot skillet. Bake for 20-25 minutes or until the cornbread is firm and the crust golden brown and crispy. Remove the skillet from the oven and serve.

Serving suggestion: Serve with broccoli cheese or potato soup. Use the cornbread instead of bread sticks or crackers with a salad. Goes well with most any main dish.

Sausage Onion Cornbread

Makes a 10" skillet

1 cup plain yellow cornmeal
1 cup all purpose flour
2 tbs. granulated sugar
2 tsp. baking powder
1 tsp. salt
1/2 tsp. baking soda
5 tbs. unsalted butter
1 cup onion, finely chopped
1 egg
1 cup whole milk
8 oz. ground pork sausage

Preheat the oven to 350°. In a 10" cast iron skillet, add the sausage and onion. Place the skillet over medium low heat and cook the sausage until it is no longer pink and done.

In a mixing bowl, add the cornmeal, all purpose flour, granulated sugar, baking powder, salt, baking soda and butter. Using your fingers, cut the butter into the dry ingredients. Add the egg and whole milk. Stir until well combined. Pour the batter over the sausage and onion in the skillet. Place the skillet in the oven and bake for 25-30 minutes or until the cornbread is done and golden brown. Remove the skillet from the oven and invert onto a serving plate.

Note: If your sausage is lean, add 2 tablespoons vegetable oil to the skillet before cooking the sausage and onion. The skillet should be well greased with sausage drippings or vegetable oil before adding the batter.

Serving suggestion: Serve with scrambled eggs and milk gravy for breakfast. Delicious with a slice of cheddar cheese and a bowl of soup or salad for lunch or dinner.

Tex Mex Cornbread

Makes a 10" skillet

1/4 cup plus 2 tablespoons vegetable oil
3 eggs
1 1/4 cups whole milk
1 cup cream style corn
2 tbs. chopped onion
2 tbs. minced jalapeno peppers
1 1/2 cups plain yellow or white cornmeal
1/4 cup all purpose flour
1 tsp. salt
2 tsp. baking powder
1/2 tsp. baking soda
1 cup shredded Pepper Jack cheese

Preheat the oven to 425°. Place 2 tablespoons vegetable oil in a 10" cast iron skillet. Heat the skillet and oil for 3-4 minutes before adding the batter.

In a mixing bowl, add 1/4 cup vegetable oil, eggs, milk, cream style corn, onion and jalapeno peppers. Whisk until well blended. Add the cornmeal, all purpose flour, salt, baking powder, baking soda and Pepper Jack cheese. Stir only until the batter is moistened.

Pour the batter into the prepared pan. Bake for 20-25 minutes or until the cornbread is firm and the crust is golden brown and crispy. Remove the cornbread from the oven and serve hot.

Serving suggestion: We serve this cornbread with beans, stews or hearty soups. It is delicious by itself or served with butter or cheddar cheese.

Jalapeno Corn Cornbread

Makes a large 12" skillet

1 1/2 cups plain yellow cornmeal
1 1/2 cups all purpose flour
3 tsp. baking powder
1/2 tsp. baking soda
3/4 tsp. salt
2 tbs. granulated sugar
4 oz. can diced green chiles, drained
1 cup cooked whole kernel corn
2 eggs
1 to 1 1/4 cups whole milk
7 tbs. vegetable oil

You can use a 10" skillet but the cornbread may overflow the skillet so place a baking pan under the skillet to prevent a mess if needed.

Preheat the oven to 425°. Grease a 12" skillet with 2 tablespoons vegetable oil. Heat the skillet and vegetable oil for 3-4 minutes before adding the batter.

In a mixing bowl, add the cornmeal, all purpose flour, baking powder, baking soda, salt, granulated sugar, green chiles and corn. Stir until well combined. Add the eggs, 5 tablespoons vegetable oil and 1 cup milk. Stir until well combined.

Every cornmeal absorbs liquids differently. Add the remaining milk if needed to make a pourable but thick batter. Pour the batter into the hot skillet.

Bake for 20-25 minutes or until the center of the cornbread is done and the crust golden brown and crispy.

Serving suggestion: Serve with brown or white beans, chili, soups or stews. Also good with a garden salad or use the cornbread as a base for tacos instead of a taco shell.

Sour Cream Cornbread

Makes a 9" skillet

2 eggs
1 cup sour cream
6 tbs. unsalted butter, melted
1/4 cup whole milk
1/2 cup all purpose flour
1 1/4 cups plain yellow or white cornmeal
1 1/2 tsp. baking powder
1/2 tsp. salt
3/4 tsp. baking soda
1 tbs. granulated sugar
1 cup whole kernel corn, cooked
2 tbs. vegetable oil

Preheat the oven to 425°. Grease a 9" cast iron skillet with 2 tablespoons vegetable oil. Heat the skillet and oil for 3-4 minutes before adding the batter.

In a mixing bowl, add the eggs, sour cream, melted butter, milk and corn. Stir until well combined. Add the all purpose flour, cornmeal, baking powder, salt, baking soda and granulated sugar. Stir only until the batter is moistened and combined.

Pour the batter into the hot skillet. Bake for 18-25 minutes or until the cornbread is firm and the crust golden brown.

Serving suggestion: Serve with potato soup, stews or any main dish instead of dinner rolls.

Chipotle Cornbread

Makes an 8" skillet

1 cup plain yellow or white cornmeal
1/2 cup all purpose flour
2 tsp. baking powder
1/4 tsp. baking soda
3/4 tsp. salt
1 cup sour cream
2 tbs. honey
1 egg
6 tbs. vegetable oil
1/2 cup chopped chipotle peppers
1/2 cup whole kernel corn

Preheat the oven to 425°. Grease an 8" cast iron skillet with 2 tablespoons vegetable oil. Heat the skillet and the oil for 3-4 minutes before adding the batter.

In a mixing bowl, add the cornmeal, all purpose flour, baking powder, baking soda and salt. Stir until well combined. Add the sour cream, honey, egg, 4 tablespoons vegetable oil, chipotle peppers and corn. Stir until well blended.

Pour the batter into the hot skillet. Bake for 18-25 minutes or until the cornbread is firm and the crust golden brown.

Serving suggestion: This cornbread is delicious with beans, greens, hearty stews and chili. Serve with butter alongside a hearty salad for a delightful lunch or dinner.

Corn Lace Cakes

Makes about 16 cakes

1/2 tsp. baking soda
1 cup buttermilk
1 egg, beaten
2/3 cup plain white cornmeal
3/4 tsp. salt
1/4 cup water
3 tbs. unsalted butter, melted

In a mixing bowl, add the baking soda, buttermilk and egg. Whisk until well combined. Add the cornmeal, salt and water. Stir until the batter is moistened.

These cakes will resemble small and thin funnel cakes. You can use a small funnel to make the cakes or I drip the batter from the end of a large spoon in a circle to make a lace design.

In a skillet over medium heat, add the butter. When the butter is hot, drop the batter as stated above into the butter. When the bubbles burst on the first side, flip the cakes over and cook on the other side. The method is similar to making pancakes. On my stove it takes about 1-2 minutes per side. Remove the cakes from the skillet and serve hot.

Serving suggestion: In my family, we like to eat them slathered in butter and serve with maple syrup and sorghum. They are equally delicious with soups and stews. Use your imagination and I am sure you will find many uses for them.

Corn Pone Bread

Makes a 10" bundt pan

2 cups self rising yellow or white cornmeal
1 cup self rising flour
1 egg
1/2 cup granulated sugar
2 cups buttermilk
1/2 cup unsalted butter, melted

Preheat the oven to 425°. Pour the melted butter in the bottom of the Bundt pan. Brush the butter up the sides of the bundt pan.

In a mixing bowl, add the cornmeal, self rising flour, egg, granulated sugar and buttermilk. Stir until well blended. Pour the batter over the butter in the pan. Do not stir. Bake for 30-40 minutes or until the bread test done in the center with a toothpick and is golden brown.

Remove the bread from the oven and let the bread cool for 5 minutes before removing from the pan. Invert the pan onto a serving plate.

You can use 1/4 cup granulated sugar if you want a less sweet bread.

Serving suggestion: Serve the bread hot with butter, jam or sorghum if desired. Delicious with beans, greens, soups, stews or chili. Serve alongside casseroles instead of rolls.

Tomato Bell Pepper Bread

Makes one loaf

3 cups all purpose flour
2 tsp. baking powder
1 1/4 tsp. salt
1 cup freshly grated Parmesan cheese
1 cup shredded sharp cheddar cheese
4 tbs. unsalted butter
4 eggs
1/2 cup whole milk
3 garlic cloves, minced
1/2 cup green bell pepper, finely chopped
1/2 cup sun dried tomatoes, finely chopped
2 tbs. unsalted butter, melted

If using sun dried tomatoes that are not packed in oil, you will need to rehydrate the tomatoes. Place 1/2 cup sun dried tomatoes in a mixing bowl. Pour 2 cups boiling water over the tomatoes. Let the tomatoes soak for 1 hour. Use as directed in the recipe.

Preheat the oven to 350°. Spray a 9" round casserole or a deep 9" cake pan with non stick cooking spray. In a mixing bowl, add the all purpose flour, baking powder, salt, Parmesan and cheddar cheese. Stir until well combined.

Using your fingers, work 4 tablespoons butter into the dry ingredients until you have crumbs. Stir in the green bell peppers and tomatoes.

In a separate bowl, add the eggs, milk and garlic. Stir until the eggs are well beaten. Add the egg mixture to the dry ingredients. Mix only until the batter is moistened and combined. Spoon the batter into the prepared pan. Bake for 35-45 minutes or until the center of the bread test done with a toothpick. Remove the bread from the oven and cool the bread for 10 minutes in the pan. Brush the top of the bread with melted butter.

Serving suggestion: Eat the bread by itself or split the bread open and use as a base for pizza. Goes well with most meats or casseroles.

Grits Bread

Makes 1 loaf

3 cups cooked grits
1 cup plain white or yellow cornmeal
1 tbs. baking powder
1/2 tsp. salt
4 eggs, beaten
1/2 cup unsalted butter, melted
1 cup cooked sausage or bacon, crumbled
1/4 to 1/2 cup whole milk
2 tbs. vegetable oil

Preheat the oven to 400°. Grease a loaf pan with the vegetable oil. In a mixing bowl, add the grits, cornmeal, baking powder, salt, eggs, butter and sausage. Stir until well combined. Only add enough milk to make a batter the consistency of thick pancake batter.

Pour the batter into the prepared pan. Bake for 45-55 minutes or until the center of the bread test done with a toothpick. Remove the pan from the oven and let the bread cool for 15 minutes before removing the bread from the pan.

This bread will be dense and resemble a spoon bread instead of a quick bread.

Serving suggestion: Serve with any meal. Toast the slices and spread with butter, jelly or sorghum for a delicious breakfast. Use the slices in place of bread for breakfast sandwiches.

3 BISCUITS

Cheddar Cheese Scones

Makes 10 scones

1 1/2 cups all purpose flour
1 1/2 cups quick oats
1/4 cup light brown sugar
1 tbs. baking powder
1 tsp. cream of tartar
1/2 tsp. salt
3/4 cup sharp cheddar cheese, shredded
2/3 cup unsalted butter, melted
1/3 cup whole milk
1 egg

Preheat the oven to 425°. Spray a baking sheet with non stick cooking spray. In a mixing bowl, add the all purpose flour, oats, brown sugar, baking powder, cream of tartar, salt and cheddar cheese. Stir until well combined.

In a separate bowl, add the melted butter, milk and egg. Whisk until well combined. Pour the wet ingredients into the dry ingredients. Stir until well combined,.

Lightly flour your work surface. Place the dough on the work surface and form into a ball. Do not knead or over work the dough. Over working the dough will make the scones tough and dry. You only want the dough to absorb enough flour so you can form the dough.

Place the dough on your baking sheet. Pat the dough down to about a 1/2" thickness. You can pat the dough into a circle or a square. With a sharp knife, cut the dough into 10 pieces. Do not separate the dough. Bake for 12-15 minutes or until the scones are done and golden brown.

Serving suggestion: These scones are great with breakfast, perfect for lunch with soup and salad or serve instead of rolls with dinner. You can add 2 tablespoons of your favorite seasonings if desired for a different flavor. If you add seasonings, add a tablespoon or two of milk to make a soft dough.

Basil Parmesan Scones

Makes 8 scones

1 1/2 cups all purpose flour
1 tbs. baking powder
1/2 tsp. salt
1/4 cup chopped pine nuts
1/4 cup freshly grated Parmesan cheese
1 tsp. dried basil
1 cup heavy whipping cream

Preheat the oven to 425°. Spray your baking sheet with non stick cooking spray. Reserve 2 tablespoons of the heavy whipping cream and set aside.

In a mixing bowl, add the all purpose flour, baking powder, salt, pine nuts, Parmesan cheese and basil. Stir until well combined. Add the remaining heavy cream. Stir only until the dough comes together and begins to form a ball. Depending upon the type of Parmesan cheese used, you may need to add a teaspoon or two of additional flour or milk to make a soft dough.

Lightly flour your work surface. Place the dough on the work surface. Softly knead the dough 3 or 4 times until it forms a soft dough. Do not over knead the dough or the scones will be tough. Place the dough on your baking sheet. Pat the dough into an 8" circle. Cut the dough into 8 wedges but do no separate the scones. Brush the reserved 2 tablespoons heavy cream over the scones. Bake for 15-18 minutes or until the scones are done and lightly browned.

Remove the pan from the oven and cut the scones again if needed. Serve hot.

Serving suggestion: Delicious with Italian meals, goat cheese or spread with cream cheese. I split the scones in half and use as a base for quick pizzas.

Onion Scones

Makes 8 scones

1 onion, chopped
2 garlic cloves, minced
1/3 cup unsalted butter
2 cups all purpose flour
2 tbs. granulated sugar
1 tbs. baking powder
1/4 tsp. black pepper
1/2 tsp. salt
1/3 cup light cream
1 egg, beaten

Preheat the oven to 400°. In a skillet over medium low heat, add the onion, garlic and butter. Saute the onion and garlic for 5 minutes. Stir constantly while cooking the onion and garlic. Remove the skillet from the heat and cool for 10 minutes.

Spray your baking pan with non stick cooking spray. In a mixing bowl, add the all purpose flour, granulated sugar, baking powder, black pepper and salt. Stir until well combined. In a separate bowl, add the egg and light cream. Whisk until well combined. Add the onion, garlic and butter from the skillet. Stir until well combined. Add the egg mixture to the dry ingredients.

Stir only until the batter is combined. Lightly flour your work surface. Place the dough on the work surface and form into an 8" circle. Place the dough on the baking sheet. Cut the circle into 8 wedges but do not separate the wedges. Bake for 12-15 minutes or until the scones are done and lightly browned.

Serving suggestion: These scones are a perfect accompaniment with soups, salads or stews. We love them with butter and served with beef and mashed potatoes.

Butter Dips

Makes 10 servings

1/3 cup unsalted butter
1 tbs. granulated sugar
3 1/2 tsp. baking powder
1 1/2 tsp. salt
1 cup whole milk
2 1/4 cups all purpose flour

Preheat the oven to 400°. In a 9 x 13 pan, add the butter. Place the pan in the oven until the butter is hot and melted.

In a mixing bowl, add the salt, granulated sugar, baking powder, all purpose flour and milk. Stir until the dough leaves the side of the bowl. Lightly flour your work surface. Place the dough on the work surface. Coat the dough with the flour on the work surface and knead the dough lightly about 10 times.

Roll the dough into a 12 x 8 rectangle about 1/2" thick. Cut the dough in half lengthwise and then cut the dough crosswise into 16 strips. Pick up each strip and roll the strip in the butter in the pan. Lay the strip in the pan and repeat with the remaining strips. Lay the strips close together in the pan. Bake for 15-20 minutes or until the bread is golden brown.

Cheese Dips: Add 1/2 cup grated sharp cheddar cheese to the batter when making the dough. Follow the recipe as directed.

Garlic Butter Dips: Add 1 clove finely minced garlic to the butter when melting. Stir the garlic into the butter before rolling the strips in the butter.

Chive Dips: Add 1/2 cup freshly minced chives to the dough before mixing. Follow the recipe as directed.

Herb Dips: Sprinkle 1 to 2 tablespoons of your favorite herbs over the strips before baking.

Serving suggestion: Use in place of rolls for any meal.

Bacon Rolls

Makes 6 servings

1 cup all purpose flour
1 tsp. baking powder
Pinch of salt
2 tbs. unsalted butter, chilled
1/2 cup whole milk
1/2 cup cooked bacon, crumbled
2 tbs. unsalted butter, melted

Preheat the oven to 400°. Spray your baking sheet with non stick cooking spray. In a mixing bowl, add the all purpose flour, baking powder and salt. Stir until well combined. Using your fingers, add the chilled butter and work the butter into the dry ingredients. You should still be able to see tiny pieces of butter when finished. Add the milk and mix only until the dough comes together and leaves the side of the bowl.

Lightly flour your work surface. Place the dough on the work surface and pat the dough into a rectangle about 1/4" thick. Sprinkle the bacon over the rectangle. Roll the dough up, starting with a long side, like you would a jelly roll.

Use a sharp knife and cut the dough into 1/2" slices. Place the slices on your baking pan. Bake for 15-18 minutes or until the rolls are done and lightly browned. Remove the rolls from the oven and brush the melted butter over the rolls before serving.

Serving suggestion: Serve for breakfast with eggs, butter and jelly. Wonderful with soups, salads and stews. Delicious with chicken dishes.

In A Hurry Cheese Crescents

Makes 10 rolls

2 cups Bisquick
1/4 to 1/2 cup whole milk
2 tbs. unsalted butter, melted
1 cup sharp cheddar cheese, shredded

Preheat the oven to 450°. Spray your baking sheet with non stick cooking spray. In a mixing bowl, add the Bisquick and 1/4 cup milk. Stir until combined. Add the remaining milk as needed to make a soft dough. Depending upon humidity, you may only need 1 or 2 tablespoons additional milk. Add a tablespoon at a time until you get the right consistency.

You need a soft dough but the dough should hold together. Lightly flour your work surface. Place the dough on the work surface. Sprinkle the dough lightly with flour if needed. Roll the dough into a 14" circle. Cut the dough into 10 wedges. Brush the dough with the melted butter. Sprinkle the cheese across the dough.

Starting with a wide end, roll the dough up like you would crescent rolls. Place the rolls on the baking sheet. Bake for 8-11 minutes or until the rolls are done and golden brown. Serve hot.

Serving suggestion: You can sprinkle garlic powder or any seasoning over the dough if desired. Serve with breakfast, lunch or dinner. The rolls are versatile and go well with most

Taco Spiced Cornmeal Biscuits

Makes 12 biscuits

1 3/4 cups all purpose flour
1/3 cup plain white cornmeal
2 1/2 tsp. baking powder
1/2 tsp. baking soda
3/4 tsp. salt
1 1/2 tbs. granulated sugar
6 tbs. cold unsalted butter
3/4 to 1 cup buttermilk
2 tsp. taco seasoning mix
1 tbs. vegetable shortening

Preheat the oven to 425°. Grease your baking pan with the vegetable shortening. In a mixing bowl, add the all purpose flour, cornmeal, baking powder, baking soda, salt, granulated sugar and taco seasoning mix. Stir until well combined.

Using your fingers, add the butter and work the butter into the dry ingredients. You should still be able to see tiny pieces of butter when finished. Add 3/4 cup milk and stir only until the dough is moistened and the dough leaves the side of the bowl. Add the remaining milk if needed to make a soft and moist dough.

Lightly flour your work surface. Place the dough on the work surface and knead the dough a couple times. Do not over work the dough or the biscuits will be tough. Pat the dough out to a 3/4" thickness.

Using a 2" round biscuit cutter, cut out the biscuits. Roll the remaining scraps of dough and cut out the remaining biscuits. Place the biscuits on the greased baking sheet with the sides touching each other. Bake for 12-15 minutes or until the biscuits are golden brown.

Brush butter across the biscuits if desired. You can substitute any herb combination for the taco seasoning if desired.

Pimento Cheese Biscuits

You can substitute 2 cups store bought pimento cheese if desired but homemade pimento cheese is so much better.

Makes 12 biscuits

2 cups shredded cheddar cheese
2 oz. jar red diced pimentos, drained well
1/3 cup mayonnaise
1/4 tsp. dry mustard
1/8 tsp. cayenne pepper
2 cups self rising flour
3/4 cup whole milk
1/4 cup vegetable shortening, cold
1 tbs. vegetable shortening

In a mixing bowl, add the cheddar cheese, pimentos, mayonnaise, dry mustard and cayenne pepper. Stir until well combined. Set the pimento cheese aside for now.

Preheat the oven to 450°. Grease your baking pan with 1 tablespoon vegetable shortening. In a mixing bowl, add the self rising flour and 1/4 cup vegetable shortening. Using your fingers, work the shortening into the flour. You should still be able to see tiny pieces of shortening when done. Add the milk and stir only until the dough is moistened and begins to leave the side of the bowl.

Lightly flour your work surface. Place the dough on the work surface. Do not add additional flour unless needed to make a soft dough that holds together. Flatten the dough with your hand. Fold the dough in half and flatten the dough again. Pat the dough into a 14 x 10 inch rectangle. Spread the pimento cheese over the dough.

Starting with a long end, roll the dough up like a jelly roll. Roll the dough tightly but not so tight as to damage the dough. Using a sharp knife, cut the dough into slices about 3/4" thick. Place the biscuits on your prepared pan with the sides touching each other. Bake for 13-16 minutes or until the biscuits are golden brown.

Blue Cheese & Olive Drop Biscuits

Makes about 16-20 small drop biscuits

2 cups self rising flour
1/4 tsp. cayenne pepper
1/4 cup vegetable shortening, chilled
1 cup crumbled blue cheese
1/4 cup Kalamata olives, diced
1 tsp. fresh thyme, minced
3/4 cup whole milk
1 tbs. vegetable shortening
2 tbs. unsalted butter, melted

Preheat the oven to 425°. Grease your baking sheet with 1 tablespoon vegetable shortening. In a mixing bowl, add the self rising flour, cayenne pepper and 1/4 cup vegetable shortening. Using your fingers, work the shortening into the flour. You should still be able to see tiny pieces of shortening when done.

Add the blue cheese, olives, thyme and milk. Stir only until the dough is moistened and combined. Drop the dough by tablespoonfuls on the prepared baking sheet. Bake for 12-15 minutes or until the biscuits are done and golden brown. Remove the biscuits from the oven and brush the melted butter across the biscuits.

Serving suggestion: Serve these biscuits for dinner in place of dinner rolls. They are excellent with soups, stews, salads or most casseroles.

Bacon, Cheddar and Tomato Biscuit Sandwiches

This is an old Southern favorite for breakfast or lunch. This biscuit is made often when the tomatoes are ripe from the garden.

Makes about 15-16 biscuits

3 cups self rising flour
6 tbs. unsalted butter, chilled
2 cups shredded cheddar cheese
10 slices bacon, cooked and crumbled
1 1/3 cups whole milk
Mayonnaise
18 slices ripe red tomato
1 tbs. vegetable shortening
2 tbs. unsalted butter, melted

Preheat the oven to 425°. Grease your baking sheet with the vegetable shortening. In a mixing bowl, add the self rising flour and 6 tablespoons butter. Using your fingers, work the butter into the flour. You should still see tiny pieces of butter when finished.

Add the cheddar cheese, bacon and milk. Stir until the dough is combined and moistened. Depending upon the dryness of the cheese, you may need to add another tablespoon or two of milk. The dough should be moist.

Using a 1/4 cup measure, scoop up the dough and place 1/4 cupfuls onto the baking sheet. Each biscuit should have about a 1/4 cupful of dough. Don't level the dough off in the cup. An estimated amount is fine to use. Pat the biscuits down slightly with lightly floured hands if desired.

Bake for 12-15 minutes or until the biscuits are done and golden brown. Remove the biscuits from the oven and brush with the melted butter. Split each biscuit open and spread with mayonnaise to your taste. Place a slice of tomato on one biscuit half. Top with the remaining biscuit half and enjoy..

Serving suggestion: You can add a slice of fried ham or sausage to the biscuit for a hearty breakfast sandwich or quick lunch or dinner.

Taco Drop Biscuits

Makes 18-22 drop biscuits

2 cups self rising flour
1/4 cup vegetable shortening
1/2 cup whole milk
1/4 cup taco sauce
1/2 cup shredded cheddar cheese
1 tsp. dried minced onion
3 tbs. unsalted butter, melted

Preheat the oven to 450°. Grease your baking sheet with 1 tablespoon melted butter. In a mixing bowl, add the self rising flour and vegetable shortening. Using your fingers, work the shortening into the flour. You should still be able to see tiny pieces of shortening when done.

Add the milk, taco sauce, cheddar cheese and onion. Stir until the dough is well combined. Drop the dough by tablespoonfuls onto your baking sheet. Bake for 8-10 minutes or until the biscuits are done and browned. Remove the biscuits from the oven and brush 2 tablespoons melted butter across the tops of the biscuits.

Serving suggestion: Serve with any Mexican meal, beans, greens, soups or stews.

Parsley Biscuits

Makes 12 biscuits

2 cups all purpose flour
1 tbs. baking powder
1/4 tsp. baking soda
3/4 tsp. salt
1 tbs. granulated sugar
1/4 cup unsalted butter
2 tbs. vegetable oil
3 tbs. fresh chopped parsley
3/4 cup whole milk
3 tbs. melted butter

Preheat the oven to 425°. Brush 1 tablespoon melted butter onto a baking pan. In a mixing bowl, add the all purpose flour, baking powder, baking soda, salt, granulated sugar and 1/4 cup butter. Using your fingers, work the butter into the dry ingredients. The dough should resemble coarse crumbs and you should still see tiny pieces of butter in the dough when done.

Add the parsley, milk and vegetable oil to the dough. Stir only until a dough forms or about 1 minute. Lightly flour your work surface. Place the dough on the work surface. Fold the dough in half and then in half again, rotating the dough slightly each time you fold. Repeat this process three or four times to form layers. Pat the dough to 3/4" thickness. Cut the biscuits out using a 2" biscuit cutter. Place the biscuits on the prepared pan.

Bake for 12-15 minutes or until the biscuits are done and golden brown. Remove the biscuits from the oven and brush with 2 tablespoons melted butter.

Serving suggestion: Serve the biscuits with any soup or stew. Delicious with chicken dishes or casseroles and most salads.

Cream Cheese and Chive Biscuits

Makes about 12 biscuits

2 1/2 cups all purpose flour
1 tbs. baking powder
1/4 tsp. baking soda
2 tsp. granulated sugar
1 tsp. salt
4 tbs. fresh minced chives
5 tbs. cold unsalted butter
4 oz. cold cream cheese
1 cup whole milk
2 tbs. unsalted butter, melted
1 tbs. vegetable shortening

Preheat the oven to 425°. Grease your baking sheet with vegetable shortening. In a mixing bowl, add the all purpose flour, baking powder, baking soda, granulated sugar, salt and chives. Stir until well combined.

Add the cream cheese and 5 tablespoons butter. Work the butter and cream cheese into the dry ingredients using your fingers. You should still be able to see tiny pieces of butter when done. Add the milk and stir only enough to moisten the dough. The dough should leave the side of the bowl when moistened.

Lightly flour your work surface. Place the dough on the work surface. Do not add additional flour unless needed to make a soft dough that holds together. Flatten the dough with your hand. Fold the dough in half and flatten the dough again. Repeat 2 more times. Do not over work the dough or the biscuits will be tough.

Pat the dough out to a 3/4" thickness. Using a 2" biscuit cutter, cut out the biscuits and place each biscuit on the baking sheet. Roll the scraps of dough again and cut out the remaining biscuits. Bake for 13-16 minutes or until the biscuits are golden brown. Remove the biscuits from the oven and brush the melted butter across the top of the biscuits.

Beer and Cheddar Biscuits

Makes 12 biscuits

2 1/4 cups all purpose flour
1 tbs. granulated sugar
1 tbs. baking powder
1/2 tsp. salt
1/2 tsp. baking soda
6 tbs. unsalted butter, cold
1 cup shredded sharp cheddar cheese
3/4 cup plus 2 tbs. stout beer
2 tbs. unsalted butter, melted
1 tbs. vegetable shortening

Preheat the oven to 425°. Grease your baking pan with the vegetable shortening. In a mixing bowl, add the all purpose flour, granulated sugar, baking powder, salt, baking soda and cheese. Stir until well combined. Add 6 tablespoons cold butter. Using your fingers, work the butter into the dough. You should still see tiny pieces of butter when done.

Add the beer and mix only until the dough leaves the side of the bowl and the dough is moistened. Lightly flour your work surface. Place the dough on the work surface. Do not add additional flour unless needed to make a soft dough that holds together. Flatten the dough with your hand. Fold the dough in half and flatten the dough again. Repeat 2 more times. Do not over work the dough or the biscuits will be tough.

Pat the dough out to a 3/4" thickness. Using a 2" biscuit cutter, cut out the biscuits and place each biscuit on the baking sheet. Roll the scraps of dough again and cut out the remaining biscuits. Bake for 13-16 minutes or until the biscuits are golden brown. Remove the biscuits from the oven and brush the melted butter across the top of the biscuits.

Serving suggestion: Serve with any soup, stew, chili, meat or casserole.

Duck Fat Biscuits

Makes 10-12 biscuits

2 1/4 cups all purpose flour
1 tbs. plus 1 tsp. baking powder
1/4 tsp. baking soda
3//4 tsp. salt
3/4 to 1 cup buttermilk
1 tbs. vegetable shortening
2 tbs. unsalted butter, melted
4 tbs. cold duck fat

Preheat the oven to 425°. Grease your baking pan with the vegetable shortening. In a mixing bowl, add the all purpose flour, baking powder, baking soda and salt. Stir until well combined.

Using your fingers, add the duck fat and work the duck fat into the dry ingredients. You should still be able to see tiny pieces of duck fat when done. Add 3/4 cup buttermilk and stir the dough only until moistened and the dough begins to leave the side of the bowl. Use the remaining buttermilk if needed to make a soft dough.

Lightly flour your work surface. Place the dough on the work surface. Do not add additional flour unless needed to make a soft dough that holds together. Flatten the dough with your hand. Fold the dough in half and flatten the dough again. Repeat 2 more times. Do not over work the dough or the biscuits will be tough.

Pat the dough out to a 3/4" thickness. Using a 2" biscuit cutter, cut out the biscuits and place each biscuit on the baking sheet. Roll the scraps of dough again and cut out the remaining biscuits. Bake for 13-16 minutes or until the biscuits are golden brown. Remove the biscuits from the oven and brush the melted butter across the top of the biscuits.

Serving suggestion: Delicious served with fried duck or chicken. The biscuits go well for breakfast or with most main dishes.

Savory Whole Wheat Biscuits

Makes about 10-12 biscuits

1 1/4 cups all purpose flour
1 cup whole wheat flour
1 tbs. baking powder
1/4 tsp. baking soda
3/4 tsp. salt
1 tbs. granulated sugar
5 tbs. unsalted butter, cold
3 green onions, chopped
2 tbs. fresh minced parsley
3/4 cup to 1 cup whole milk or buttermilk
1 tbs. vegetable shortening
2 tbs. unsalted butter, melted

Preheat the oven to 425°. Grease your baking pan with the vegetable shortening. In a mixing bowl, add the all purpose flour, whole wheat flour, baking powder, baking soda, salt, granulated sugar, green onions and parsley. Stir until well combined.

Using your fingers, add 5 tablespoons butter and work the butter into the dry ingredients. You should still be able to see tiny pieces of butter when done. Add 3/4 cup milk and mix only until the dough is moistened and begins to leave the side of the bowl. Add the remaining milk if needed to make a soft dough.

Lightly flour your work surface. Place the dough on the work surface. Do not add additional flour unless needed to make a soft dough that holds together. Flatten the dough with your hand. Fold the dough in half and flatten the dough again. Repeat 2 more times. Do not over work the dough or the biscuits will be tough.

Pat the dough out to a 3/4" thickness. Using a 2" biscuit cutter, cut out the biscuits and place each biscuit on the baking sheet. Roll the scraps of dough again and cut out the remaining biscuits. Bake for 13-16 minutes or until the biscuits are golden brown. Remove the biscuits from the oven and brush 2 tablespoons melted butter across the top of the biscuits.

Savory Pumpkin Biscuits

Makes about 12 biscuits

2 1/3 cups all purpose flour
1 tbs. baking powder
1/4 tsp. baking soda
1/2 tsp. salt
1/8 tsp. cayenne pepper
6 tbs. cold unsalted butter
1 cup pureed cooked pumpkin
1/3 cup whole milk
2 tbs. light brown sugar
1 tbs. vegetable shortening
2 tbs. unsalted butter, melted

Preheat the oven to 425°. Grease your baking pan with the vegetable shortening. In a mixing bowl, add the all purpose flour, baking powder, baking soda, salt, cayenne pepper and brown sugar. Stir until well mixed. The brown sugar must be well combined in the dry ingredients.

Add 6 tablespoons cold butter. Using your fingers, work the butter into the dry ingredients. You should still see tiny pieces of butter when done. Add the pumpkin and milk. Mix only until the dough is moistened and combined.

Lightly flour your work surface. Place the dough on the work surface. Do not add additional flour unless needed to make a soft dough that holds together. Flatten the dough with your hand. Fold the dough in half and flatten the dough again. Repeat 2 more times. Do not over work the dough or the biscuits will be tough.

Pat the dough out to a 3/4" thickness. Using a 2" biscuit cutter, cut out the biscuits and place each biscuit on the baking sheet. Roll the scraps of dough again and cut out the remaining biscuits. Bake for 13-16 minutes or until the biscuits are golden brown. Remove the biscuits from the oven and brush 2 tablespoons melted butter across the top of the biscuits.

Serving suggestion: Serve with butter or orange marmalade if desired. This biscuit goes well with most any main dish, soup or stew.

Browned Butter and Sage Biscuits

Makes about 12 biscuits

6 tbs. unsalted butter
2 tbs. fresh sage, chopped
1 tsp. fresh thyme, chopped
2 cups all purpose flour
1 tbs. baking powder
1 tbs. granulated sugar
3/4 tsp. salt
3/4 cup whole milk
2 tbs. unsalted butter, melted
1 tbs. vegetable shortening

Run about 3" cold water in your sink. It is very important to brown the butter for the biscuits but do not burn the butter. There is a fine line between browned butter and burnt butter so watch the cooking closely.

In a heavy sauce pan over medium heat, add 6 tablespoons butter. Stir constantly and let the butter melt. The butter will begin to brown on the bottom or the sides of the pan when ready. This will only take a couple of minutes so watch the butter closely. When the butter begins to brown, remove the pan from the heat and place the pan in the cold water. Add the sage and thyme. Let the herbs steep in the butter and cool the butter to room temperature.

Preheat the oven to 425°. Grease your baking pan with the vegetable shortening. In a mixing bowl, add the all purpose flour, baking powder, granulated sugar and salt. Stir until well combined. Add the butter and herbs along with the milk. Stir only until the dough is moistened and combined.

Browned Butter and Sage Biscuits cont'd

Lightly flour your work surface. Place the dough on the work surface. Do not add additional flour unless needed to make a soft dough that holds together. Flatten the dough with your hand. Fold the dough in half and flatten the dough again. Repeat 2 more times. Do not over work the dough or the biscuits will be tough. Pat the dough out to a 3/4" thickness. Using a 2" biscuit cutter, cut out the biscuits and place each biscuit on the baking sheet. Roll the scraps of dough again and cut out the remaining biscuits. Bake for 13-16 minutes or until the biscuits are golden brown. Remove the biscuits from the oven and brush the melted butter across the top of the biscuits.

Serving suggestion: Serve with most any chicken, turkey or wild fowl dish. The biscuits pair well with salads or stews.

Country Ham and Cheese Biscuits

Makes 12 biscuits

2 cups self rising flour
1/4 cup vegetable shortening, cold
1 cup finely chopped country ham
1 cup shredded Swiss cheese
1 cup sour cream
1/4 cup whole milk
2 tbs. unsalted butter, melted
1 tbs. vegetable shortening

Preheat the oven to 450°. Grease your baking pan with 1 tablespoon vegetable shortening. In a mixing bowl, add the self rising flour and 1/4 cup vegetable shortening. Using your fingers, work the shortening into the flour. You should still be able to see tiny pieces of shortening when done.

Add the ham, Swiss cheese, sour cream and milk. Mix only until the dough is combined and the dough begins to leave the side of the bowl.

Lightly flour your work surface. Place the dough on the work surface. Do not add additional flour unless needed to make a soft dough that holds together. Flatten the dough with your hand. Fold the dough in half and flatten the dough again. Repeat 2 more times. Do not over work the dough or the biscuits will be tough.

Pat the dough out to a 3/4" thickness. Using a 2" biscuit cutter, cut out the biscuits and place each biscuit on the baking sheet. Roll the scraps of dough again and cut out the remaining biscuits. Bake for 13-16 minutes or until the biscuits are golden brown. Remove the biscuits from the oven and brush the melted butter across the top of the biscuits.

Serving suggestion: Serve as is for breakfast along with fruit and yogurt for a quick on the go breakfast. My boys like these served with pork chops and gravy. I like to eat them for lunch with a salad and iced tea.

Green Onion and Cheese Filled Cornmeal Biscuits

Makes 12 biscuits

1 1/2 cups all purpose flour
1/2 cup plain white or yellow cornmeal
1 tbs. baking powder
1/2 tsp. salt
1/3 cup cold vegetable shortening
1/2 cup sour cream
1/2 cup whole milk
4 oz. cheddar cheese block, cut into 12 cubes
2 tbs. chopped green onions
2 tbs. unsalted butter, melted
1 tbs. vegetable shortening

Preheat the oven to 450°. Grease your baking pan with 1 tablespoon vegetable shortening. In a mixing bowl, add the all purpose flour, cornmeal, baking powder, salt and green onions. Stir until well combined.

Add 1/3 cup cold vegetable shortening. Using your fingers, cut the shortening into the dry ingredients. You should still see tiny pieces of shortening when done. Add the milk and sour cream. Stir only until the dough is moistened and combined.

Lightly flour your work surface. Place the dough on the work surface. Do not add additional flour unless needed to make a soft dough that holds together. Flatten the dough with your hand. Fold the dough in half and flatten the dough again. Repeat 2 more times. Do not over work the dough or the biscuits will be tough.

Pat the dough out to a 3/4" thickness. Using a 2" biscuit cutter, cut out the biscuits and place each biscuit on the baking sheet. Roll the scraps of dough again and cut out the remaining biscuits. Stuff a cheese cube in the center of each biscuit. Bake for 13-16 minutes or until the biscuits are golden brown. Remove the biscuits from the oven and brush the melted butter across the top of the biscuits.

Ham & Cheese Biscuits

Makes 12 biscuits

2 cups all purpose flour
2 tsp. baking powder
1 tsp. baking soda
1/2 tsp. salt
1/8 tsp. dry mustard
1/8 tsp. onion powder
4 tbs. unsalted butter, cold
1/2 cup cooked finely diced ham
1/2 cup shredded cheddar cheese
1 cup whole milk
2 tbs. unsalted butter, melted
1 tbs. vegetable shortening

Preheat the oven to 450°. Grease your baking sheet with the vegetable shortening. In a mixing bowl, add the all purpose flour, baking powder, baking soda, salt, dry mustard and onion powder. Stir until well combined.

Using your fingers, add 4 tablespoons butter and work the butter into the dry ingredients. You should still see tiny pieces of butter when done. Add the ham, cheese and milk. Stir only until the dough is moistened and combined. You may need to add a tablespoon or two of additional milk to make a moist dough.

Lightly flour your work surface. Place the dough on the work surface. Do not add additional flour unless needed to make a soft dough that holds together. Flatten the dough with your hand. Fold the dough in half and flatten the dough again. Repeat 2 more times. Do not over work the dough or the biscuits will be tough.

Pat the dough out to a 3/4" thickness. Using a 2" biscuit cutter, cut out the biscuits and place each biscuit on the baking sheet. Roll the scraps of dough again and cut out the remaining biscuits. Bake for 13-16 minutes or until the biscuits are golden brown. Remove the biscuits from the oven and brush the melted butter across the top of the biscuits.

Honey Mustard Biscuits with Ham

Makes 12 biscuits

3 cups self rising flour
2/3 cup whole milk
1/2 cup unsalted butter, cold
1/4 cup Dijon honey mustard
1 1/2 lbs. ham slices, cooked
2 tbs. unsalted butter, melted
1 tbs. vegetable shortening

Preheat the oven to 450°. Grease your baking sheet with the vegetable shortening. In a mixing bowl, add the self rising flour and 1/2 cup butter. Using your fingers, work the butter into the flour. You should still be able to see tiny pieces of butter when done.

Add the milk and honey mustard. Stir until the dough is moistened and begins to leave the side of the bowl. Lightly flour your work surface. Place the dough on the work surface. Do not add additional flour unless needed to make a soft dough that holds together. Flatten the dough with your hand. Fold the dough in half and flatten the dough again. Repeat 2 more times. Do not over work the dough or the biscuits will be tough.

Pat the dough out to a 3/4" thickness. Using a 2" biscuit cutter, cut out the biscuits and place each biscuit on the baking sheet. Roll the scraps of dough again and cut out the remaining biscuits. Bake for 13-16 minutes or until the biscuits are golden brown. Remove the biscuits from the oven and brush the melted butter across the top of the biscuits.

Split the biscuits open and serve with ham slices for a biscuit sandwich.

Serving suggestion: You can replace the ham with any meat you desire. I like to add a sliced tomato to the biscuit for extra goodness. These biscuits are great with a slice of cheddar or with a salad or soup.

Bacon Ranch Biscuits

Makes about 12-16 biscuits

3 cups all purpose flour
2 1/2 tsp. baking powder
1/2 tsp. baking soda
1 tsp. salt
2 tbs. onion powder
1/2 tsp. garlic powder
2 tbs. fresh minced chives
1/2 cup unsalted butter, cold
3/4 cup crumbled and cooked bacon
1 egg
1 cup buttermilk
1 tbs. granulated sugar
1 tbs. vegetable shortening
2 tbs. unsalted butter, melted

Preheat the oven to 425°. Grease your baking pan with vegetable shortening. In a mixing bowl, add the all purpose flour, baking powder, baking soda, salt, onion powder, garlic powder, bacon, granulated sugar and chives. Stir until well blended.

Using your fingers, add the 1/2 cup cold butter. Work the butter into the dry ingredients until you only see tiny pieces of the butter.

In a separate bowl, add the egg and buttermilk. Mix until well combined. Pour the egg and buttermilk into the dry ingredients. Mix only until the dough is moistened and combined.

Lightly flour your work surface. Place the dough on the work surface. Do not add additional flour unless needed to make a soft dough that holds together. Flatten the dough with your hand. Fold the dough in half and flatten the dough again. Repeat 2 more times. Do not over work the dough or the biscuits will be tough.

Bacon Ranch Biscuits cont'd

Pat the dough out to a 3/4" thickness. Using a 2" biscuit cutter, cut out the biscuits and place each biscuit on the baking sheet. Roll the scraps of dough again and cut out the remaining biscuits. Bake for 16-20 minutes or until the biscuits are golden brown. Remove the biscuits from the oven and brush the melted butter across the top of the biscuits.

Serving suggestion: Delicious as a breakfast sandwich with eggs and cheese. Serve with most any soup or salad for a hearty meal. Delicious by themselves spread with herb cream cheese or herb butters.

Cracklin' Biscuits

Makes 12 biscuits

2 cups self rising flour
1/3 cup unsalted butter, cold
1/2 cup cracklin's
3/4 to 1 cup whole milk
2 tbs. unsalted butter, melted
1 tbs. vegetable shortening

Preheat the oven to 425°. Grease your baking sheet with 1 tablespoon vegetable shortening. In a mixing bowl, add the self rising flour and 1/3 cup butter. Using your fingers, work the butter into the flour. You should still be able to see tiny pieces of butter when done. Add the cracklin's and stir.

Add 3/4 cup milk and stir only until the batter is moistened and combined. Add the remaining milk if needed to make a soft dough.

Lightly flour your work surface. Place the dough on the work surface. Do not add additional flour unless needed to make a soft dough that holds together. Flatten the dough with your hand. Fold the dough in half and flatten the dough again. Repeat 2 more times. Do not over work the dough or the biscuits will be tough.

Pat the dough out to a 3/4" thickness. Using a 2" biscuit cutter, cut out the biscuits and place each biscuit on the baking sheet. Roll the scraps of dough again and cut out the remaining biscuits. Bake for 13-16 minutes or until the biscuits are golden brown. Remove the biscuits from the oven and brush the melted butter across the top of the biscuits.

Serving suggestion: Use the biscuits to serve with any meal. They are delicious for breakfast with butter and syrup or they go well with main dishes, casseroles, hearty soups, beans and greens.

Sage & Cheddar Cornmeal Biscuits

Makes 12 biscuits

1 1/2 cups all purpose flour
1/2 cup self rising cornmeal
2 tsp. granulated sugar
3/4 tsp. rubbed sage
2 tsp. baking powder
1/2 tsp. salt
1/2 cup vegetable shortening, cold
3/4 to 1 cup whole milk
1/2 cup shredded sharp cheddar cheese
2 tbs. unsalted butter, melted
1 tbs. vegetable shortening

Preheat the oven to 425°. Grease your baking sheet with 1 tablespoon vegetable shortening. In a mixing bowl, add the all purpose flour, cornmeal, granulated sugar, sage, baking powder and salt. Stir until well blended.

Add the vegetable shortening to the dry ingredients. Using your fingers, work the vegetable shortening into the dry ingredients. Add 3/4 cup milk and the cheddar cheese. Stir only until the dough is moistened and combined. Add the remaining milk if needed to make a soft dough.

Lightly flour your work surface. Place the dough on the work surface. Do not add additional flour unless needed to make a soft dough that holds together. Flatten the dough with your hand. Fold the dough in half and flatten the dough again. Repeat 2 more times. Do not over work the dough or the biscuits will be tough.

Pat the dough out to a 3/4" thickness. Using a 2" biscuit cutter, cut out the biscuits and place each biscuit on the baking sheet. Roll the scraps of dough again and cut out the remaining biscuits. Bake for 13-16 minutes or until the biscuits are golden brown. Remove the biscuits from the oven and brush the melted butter across the top of the biscuits.

Southern Homemade Biscuits

Makes about 10-12 biscuits

1/2 cup cold unsalted butter
3 tsp. baking powder
1/2 tsp. salt
2 cups all purpose flour
1 tsp. sugar
3/4 – 1 cup whole milk
2 tbs. melted unsalted butter
1 tbs. vegetable shortening

Preheat the oven to 450°. The oven should heat at least 10 minutes before placing the biscuits in the oven. Lightly grease your baking pan with the vegetable shortening. The closer biscuits are together in a pan, the better they will rise. Try not to use a larger than necessary pan.

In a mixing bowl, add the all purpose flour, baking powder, salt and the granulated sugar. Stir to combine. Cut 1/2 cup cold butter into small squares. With your fingers or a pastry blender, cut the butter into the flour mixture until the butter is no larger than small peas. You should be able to see the butter in the dough after you have finished cutting in the butter.

Add 3/4 cup milk and stir until the dough leaves the sides of the bowl and begins to hold together. You may need to add the additional 1/4 cup milk to make a soft dough. The dough will be soft and slightly sticky.

Turn the dough onto a floured surface. I do not use a rolling pin. Pat the dough into a circle with your hands about 1/2" thick. Add just enough flour to keep the dough from sticking to your hands. Fold the dough in half and then in half again, rotating the dough slightly each time you fold. Repeat this process four times to form layers. Pat the dough to 1/2" thickness on a floured board.

Southern Homemade Biscuits cont'd

Using a sharp 2 1/2" biscuit cutter, cut the dough into biscuits. Do not twist the biscuit cutter when cutting out the dough. Press straight down on the biscuit cutter. Cut the biscuits close together so you can cut out as many as possible on the first rolling. Place the cut biscuits on a baking sheet with the sides of each biscuit touching. Flatten out the remaining dough and repeat the cutting process until all of the dough is used.

Brush the biscuits with 1 tablespoon of the melted butter and place them in the freezer for 5 minutes. Remove the biscuits from the freezer and place the biscuits in a hot oven for 12-15 minutes. Bake the biscuits until they are golden brown and the insides are fluffy. Depending upon your oven, it may take an additional few minutes. I know it is tempting to open the oven door to see the biscuits rise, but do not open the oven before 10 minutes.

When the biscuits are done, remove them from the oven and brush the top and sides with the remaining melted butter.

Note: Add 2 teaspoons of your favorite herb combinations for different flavor biscuits.

Serving suggestion: Serve these biscuits with butter, jelly, soups, salads, stews, main dishes, fried chicken or casseroles.

TABLE OF CONTENTS

Muffins

Quick Breads

Bacon Egg & Cheese Spoon Bread, 38
Chili Pepper Parmesan Spoon Bread, 39
Southern Hush Puppies, 40
Sweet Potato Hush Puppies, 41
Beer Batter Hush Puppies, 42
Parmesan Herb Quick Bread, 43
Quick Herb Batter Bread, 44
Fresh Dill Beer Bread, 45
Beer Bread, 46
Bacon, Onion & Kale Bread, 47
Bacon Cheese Bread, 48
Green Chile Cheese Popcorn Bread, 49
Dill Pickle Bread, 50
Cheddar Squash Bread, 51
Ham & Cheese Olive Loaf, 52
Tabasco Onion Cheese Bread, 53
Spinach Garlic Quick Bread, 54
Green Onion Bread, 55
Olive Quick Bread, 56
Black Pepper Cheddar Bread, 57
Green Bell Pepper Quick Bread, 58
Tomato Cilantro Quick Bread, 59
Savory Swiss Olive Bread, 60
Sage Cornbread, 61
Salsa Cornbread, 62
Onion Cornbread, 63
Butternut Squash Cornbread, 64
Cheddar Bacon Cornbread, 65
Southern Breakfast Cornbread, 66
Broccoli Cornbread, 67
Sausage Onion Cornbread, 68
Tex Mex Cornbread, 69
Jalapeno Corn Cornbread, 70
Sour Cream Cornbread, 71
Chipotle Cornbread, 72
Corn Lace Cakes, 73
Corn Pone Bread, 74
Tomato Bell Pepper Bread, 75
Grits Bread, 76

Biscuits

ABOUT THE AUTHOR

Lifelong southerner who lives in Bowling Green, KY. Priorities in life are God, family and pets. I love to cook, garden and feed most any stray animal that walks into my yard. I love old cookbooks and cookie jars. Huge NBA fan who loves to spend hours watching basketball games. Enjoy cooking for family and friends and hosting parties and reunions. Can't wait each year to build gingerbread houses for the kids.

Made in the USA
Middletown, DE
03 January 2023

21212030R00071